WORK–LIFE
BRILLIANCE

Tools to **Break Stress** and Create
the **Life & Health** You Crave

Denise R. Green

Published 2017

ISBN: 978-0-692-90172-4
Brilliance Publishing

Cover Design: Sagar Heerani
Design Editing: Angela Lauria
Editing: Julia Kellaway
Interior Design: Susana Cardona
Author photo courtesy of Ultraspective Photography, Livermore, CA

Printed by CreateSpace, An Amazon.com Company

Contents

Advance Praise

"I loved this book! Denise's ability to inspire with her own journey of transformation and to offer effective brain changing strategies in her coaching is exceptional in the world of self-help books. *Work–Life Brilliance* is simply brilliant!"

—Dr. Amy Banks,
author of *Wired to Connect: The Surprising Link Between Brain Science and Strong, Healthy Relationships*

"As a technology executive with two teenaged daughters and an overfull life, the book really spoke to me. Denise 'gets it' and her practical, clear, and insightful approach will help you shift a 'crazy-busy life' to an 'abundantly brilliant life.'"

—Kirsten Wolberg,
recovering/former CIO and current Board Director

"There are some books that I wish I had written. This is one of them. Denise has written an inspired book; inspired by her credibility, inspired by her heart, and inspired by her passion. Brilliant."

—Phil Dixon,
MSc., CEO, Academy of Brain-based Leadership

"You will see yourself in this book's stories, revel in the inspiring quotes, gain confidence in the tools and advice, and benefit from the lasting positive impact on your life. A book filled with authentic truths."

—Jan Hier-King, co-founder, Bicycle Financial

This book is for Katarina,
the brightest light in my world

Foreword

As I wrote in *Fierce Conversations*, we don't burn out because we're trying to solve problems. We burn out because we've been trying to solve the same problem over and over. Guess what! Stress is a perpetual problem that most people have not been able to solve . . . and they certainly won't solve it by seeking the much-ballyhooed notion of work–life balance. While we all want to avoid burnout and feel less stressed, there is something far more profound that we seek, and which Denise addresses brilliantly in this marvelous book.

I met Denise more than a decade ago, when she was a Director of Leadership Development at Charles Schwab. After reading *Fierce Conversations*, she sought me out, and we began a journey working together to help a team of fifty executives create a culture of courageous, open, safe leadership, where anything could be discussed with heart and grace, for the good of the organization and the thousands of souls working in it. Denise writes like she speaks and coaches: to the whole person—with deep compassion, wit, creativity, wisdom, and urgency. She gets what it's like to have a yearning to be your best self, while constrained by the realities of demanding jobs, stress, and even physical injury and illness. This is not a book to be read casually; it's a book to be consumed. Denise offers a lifeline here, out of whatever swamp of the soul you find yourself in, to your best self.

I'm known for asking, "What are you pretending not to know?" I've never seen a tool that answers this more effectively and efficiently than Denise's *Brilliant Life Assessment.* It reaches into your subconscious and presents the answer visually on paper in about five minutes. This new, old knowledge frees you to let go of the toxic "should-dos" on your list and focus on what matters most—to your soul—right now. Then, Denise walks you through a process to realize your goal. Page after page, Denise offers profound insights and simple tools to turn your epiphanies into real progress.

This book is a fierce, loving, convincing, and oh-so-very-useful conversation between you and Denise. I suggest you listen. Life's too short (and your potential is too big) not to.

SUSAN SCOTT, author of *Fierce Conversations: Achieving Success at Work & in Life—One Conversation at a Time* and *Fierce Leadership: A Bold Alternative to the Worst "Best" Practices of Business Today*

Introduction

I recently caught up with my colleague and friend Rachel, whom I'd been worried about. It had been a couple of months since we connected, and the last time I saw her, she was working at such a frantic pace, in charge of so many projects, I wondered how long she could keep it up. Her responses to e-mails went from a turnaround time of about twenty-four hours, to a week, then two weeks, then never. Rachel is so good at her job that people come to her constantly for advice. She always makes time for people, despite the fact that it throws her calendar into chaos and has her pushing work into the evening hours. She's a visionary thinker who often comes up with exciting projects that add to her already full plate. She agreed to take on a second job temporarily while leadership searched for her new manager. Months later, they hired someone from outside the company. Given his steep learning curve, her "temporary" second job continued and, despite her request for support, looked like it was hers indefinitely.

When I met her for lunch, I was stunned by the shift in her—she was smiling, relaxed, and radiant. Our meeting was supposed to be a quick one where we discussed a long list of work items. Instead, we had a leisurely two-hour lunch where we talked about life, health, travel, and eventually, wrapped up loose ends on our projects. What had changed? Rachel began our meeting by telling me that three weeks prior, she was in a senior leadership meeting when suddenly, her throat began itching and her tongue swelled. She was having trouble breathing, and silently began panicking. She left the meeting, called the medical hotline, and described what was happening. They said they'd send an ambulance right away but Rachel told them not to (she didn't want to make a scene) and that she could get there faster on her own. When she arrived in the ER, they triaged and admitted her immediately. She was in anaphylactic shock, despite having no known allergies. If she'd waited an hour longer, she may have died. They ran tests and concluded that Rachel was the victim of stress overload; her body had finally burned out.

Rachel had known that she was on the wrong trajectory. She'd even told her boss she needed help, but he was overwhelmed and didn't recognize the gravity of her situation. Rachel could have taken medical leave after this incident, but in true form, she came back to work after a weekend of rest. She went straight to her department head and told him that she wanted to work, but under different terms. As a result, her "temporary" job was lifted off her shoulders.

When we met three weeks later, she was beaming. She'd lost a few pounds without even trying, she was working on projects that were in her sweet spot, she was sleeping until 7:00 AM, arriving at work by 9:00 AM (whereas before she was in the office by 7:30 AM), and she was excited about taking a two-week cruise in the Mediterranean. The irony of our times is that, while technology has enabled us to have freedoms that were once unimaginable—appliances that save us from hand-washing clothes, an Internet that helps us communicate efficiently, smartphones that help us work from anywhere so we aren't tethered to an office, streaming entertainment that we can customize to our schedule—it's also created a "constantly on" environment where we actually have less free time than people had a hundred years ago. We are designed for burnout.

And, as we'll learn in later chapters, it's incredibly hard to resist piling on more—more work, more activities, more getting hooked by our screens—so we end up having less space to just be. And for parents, it's more challenging than ever to create time to be present with our children in meaningful ways. No one is immune to stress, and the first steps toward burnout are happening at a younger age than ever. Children and adults alike are over-scheduled, under-rested, and frazzled. We need coping strategies—good ones. I once worked with a senior leader whose strategy for dealing with constant back-to-back meetings included never drinking water (so she didn't have to take a pee break), and working at home until midnight.

There are better antidotes.

Why I Wrote this Book

I'm on a mission to help people light the spark within them that may feel like it's been nearly snuffed out due to the demands of life. I don't work for the UN, Peace Corps, Oxfam, or other noble organization; the world I come from—and that I aim to heal—is corporate America. I know what it's like to spend much of your life in meetings or in front of e-mail, sitting (and sitting, and sitting) under florescent lights, amidst too much air conditioning and too little fresh air. And I know what it's like to work from home and try to take calls while the dog is barking at the mailman and your child ignores your closed office door, knocking anyway. I know what it's like to have your body crash and burn so hard you wonder if you'll ever feel like yourself again. I know what it's like to have to put a smile on your face and try to act with grace while you're dealing with the weight of personal tragedy. And I know what it's like to feel like your soul is slowly withering and that there must be a better way. And I know, as deeply as one can, what it feels like to doubt that you will ever live into your full potential. I also know the way out.

For over a decade, I've helped managers and leaders redesign their lives and health for the better, which always leads to better performance at work. Usually, they come to me just before their breaking point. Any shame they feel for not being able to "have it all" with grace and ease usually gets lifted when they learn just how normal their situation is.

If you feel stuck, that's okay. In fact, the more pain you feel now, the more you're ready for this book and the tools I have outlined inside. I often recall Dante's design for hell, where the only way out was through Satan's butthole: talk about hitting rock bottom.

Regardless of the circle of hell you find yourself in, this book can pull you out. I've helped thousands of people make small changes for big results, and I've created this book so you can access the pragmatic and transformational tools I use with my clients every day.

And if you find yourself not in hell—but in your own personal purgatory—where you have no major complaints, but life is just okay (or "blah," as I call the halfway point between burned out and brilliant), you'll find tools and insights in this book that will help you create a vibrantly fulfilling life.

How to Use this Book

The purpose of this book is to help you unearth your most brilliant self—one tiny step at a time. And just to be clear, when I say "brilliant," I'm not talking about intelligence or Guinness beer commercials. I'm referring to the light within all of us that's been dimmed over the years, and that has you feeling the way you're feeling now. We'll talk more about what brilliance looks like in the chapters that follow.

While human needs are somewhat universal, your situation, challenges, and solutions are unique. My process and tools work for anyone and will help you get clear about what exactly would be the best investment of your precious time and focus. I never know what my clients will present as challenges, and I love tailoring approaches that are just right for each individual. I designed this book to let you do the same. You don't have to know *what* to change, nor *how*. We'll get there. And if you do already know what has to change, feel free to skip to the chapter that's most relevant for you.

I'll offer proven, pragmatic action steps that will help you rewire your brain and your life for the better. Sure, you can skip the reflection and planning exercises and just read leisurely. But if you do, I suggest you come back to them after you've let the concepts simmer enough and you feel ready to start. Then do the exercises that are most relevant. If you don't, you'll be like a well-read inmate: smarter, but still trapped.

PART ONE is the "What and Why" section of the book that sets the foundation for all that follows. I invite you to read this section and reflect without committing to any changes. Just come along on the ride with me, and when prompted, take a moment to jot down reflections that will make the content real and useful to you.

PART TWO is the "How" section of the book, where you'll learn the exact steps you must take—and what pitfalls to avoid—if you're going to change any part of your life. You'll discover the common mistakes nearly everyone makes when they're trying to achieve a goal or change a habit, and you'll feel confident that this time will be different because you now know the tricks. I'll help you choose a focus area using my efficient and enlightening Brilliant Life Assessment, and you'll be able to make real progress on that area before you even finish the book.

And, if ever the book doesn't seem like enough, and you need a real live human conversation, I'm just an e-mail away at Denise@BrillianceInc.com.

My Commitment to You

Stress presents itself in numerous ways including weight gain, eye-twitching, mood swings, shortness of breath, anxiety, and eventually, major health breakdowns. If you've experienced none of those symptoms, you must be my mom, and you're only reading this because you're so darn proud of me. If you're not my mom, and they still don't apply . . . you're probably reading the wrong book. Go grab a *People* magazine, spy thriller, or whatever else floats your boat and congratulate yourself on creating a life of joy, meaning, and ease (or denial—that works too for a while).

For the rest of you, because you're already so damn busy, I make the following commitments:

- I'll respect your time: the tools in this book are designed to help in only a few minutes.
- I'll give you only enough theory and brain science to provide you with useful context. (Lucky for you, my degrees are in languages and liberal arts, so how sidetracked can I get?)
- I'll walk you step-by-step through the process of choosing a focus area and making real progress, so you feel guided and supported, with a deep sense that you can take small actions that will make a positive difference.
- I won't take it personally if you skip around in the book and go to sections that feel most important to you right now, grabbing a few tips that will help immediately.

Let's begin!

With love and light,

Denise

*The journey of a thousand miles
begins with a single step.*

—Lao Tzu

PART ONE:

WHY AND WHAT?

CHAPTER ONE:

Burnout versus Brilliance

If I manage to survive the week, I want a straightjacket in hot pink and my helmet to sparkle.

—seen on Pinterest

The Stress Epidemic

Ellen is a director at a multibillion-dollar health company. She wanted me to help her learn to delegate better so she could develop her people and free up time in her calendar. Like so many of my clients, Ellen was extremely good at what she did—in her case, implementing complex, multimillion-dollar technology build-outs in new medical and corporate facilities. She was the voice they wanted in all the meetings, and the person to go to with crises. She struggled to please both her clients on the technology side and management on the facilities side. To make matters more complicated, her organization was going through a painful restructure and she had no direct boss. Then, just when she thought it couldn't get more challenging, a toxic and insecure leader was appointed to the senior position, despite having no managerial experience. Ellen's sixty-hour workweeks became even longer and more stressful. She barely saw her family, worked weekends, and was consumed with anxiety and guilt for neglecting her employees, her kids, and her now pointless gym membership. Her weight ballooned and she developed an eye twitch. Sadly, Ellen's story isn't unusual.

If you sometimes feel overwhelmed, stressed, or anxious, you're in good company. A 2014 landmark study of seven-thousand doctors and other workers led by Dr. Tait Shanafelt of the Mayo Clinic characterized burnout as comprising these traits: emotional exhaustion, bitter cynicism, a plummeting sense of accomplishment, and "a tendency to view people as objects rather than as human beings." As an executive coach, I'm privileged to partner with incredibly intelligent, ambitious, heartfelt people who are committed to working with me to improve their performance and their lives on every level. From the outside looking in, these people appear to have it all. And yet, as their confidant, I know that they suffer. Whether you suffer from all the official symptoms of burnout (or BO as I affectionately call it), or just one or two, it's time to get help now.

Most people get a coach when they're close to their breaking point. In the past year alone, I've worked with people who are experiencing anxiety, insomnia, interpersonal conflicts at work and home, guilt about spending too little time with family and friends, weight gain, eye twitching, autoimmune disorders, diabetes, and heart attack.

Many of my clients don't present stress as the topic for coaching. Some reasons include:

- they believe they can't be successful without feeling fried;
- they think it's impossible to live life with ease given all the demands on them;
- they think it sounds weak to complain about stress; or,
- they're so used to feeling stressed, they don't even know how close they are to breaking.

They're like the proverbial frog in increasingly hot water, unaware that they're about to be cooked.

The truth is, high stress will prevent you from attaining and sustaining high performance; it's physically impossible to be your best when you experience great amounts of stress. I'm on a mission to help people suffering from burnout bring ease back into their lives, so they can be their most brilliant selves. And I know from experience what that feels like. I used to think I was immune to stress, but I was clearly in denial. After severe stress and sleep deprivation during the year after my daughter's birth, I was diagnosed with post-traumatic stress disorder (PTSD). I was so shocked that I sought a second opinion. Again, I was diagnosed with PTSD. I eventually healed my brain—and you can too, no matter how burned out you are.

Throughout this book, I'll share my favorite techniques for reducing stress so you can rediscover your best self.

THE NATURE OF STRESS

First, the good news about stress: unless you aspire to be a bored underachiever, some amount of stress is useful. In order to feel a sense of ease and flow—where time seems to pass by quickly—we need to feel somewhat challenged. Too little challenge or stress and we feel apathy. But the bad news is that *too much stress will break you*. More bad news: our jobs, workplaces, modern lives, habits, and gadgets have pushed most of us into the red danger zone—and we remain in that state almost constantly.

A MODERN PHENOMENON

We simply weren't designed for modern life. Our brains are still running on a hundred-thousand-year-old operating system that hasn't been upgraded to deal with our twenty-four-seven schedules. We were, and still are, designed to be outside, on the move, and sleeping one-third of our lives. As John Medina, author of *Brain Rules*, writes, "Our evolutionary ancestors walked about twelve miles a day. If we sat around the Serengeti for eight hours—heck, for eight minutes—we were usually somebody's lunch." Our contemporary lifestyles—especially if you work in an office—are unsuited to our human nature. Sitting in traffic and at a desk—constantly bombarded by e-mail, texts, instant messages, and office politics—all create a perfect storm for stress.

Yes, our ancestors experienced stress, but it was intermittent stress. When danger was present, the "fight-or-flight" part of our autonomic nervous system (ANS)—the sympathetic nervous system (SNS)—would take over, channeling resources away from the brain and toward muscles, helping them fire so they could "get the hell out of Dodge" in a hurry. In our modern sedentary times, our brains can't tell the difference between a hungry lion and a boss's e-mail requesting a project status update. Rather than turn on rarely and temporarily, our SNS works overtime, like a muscle that's permanently contracted. The only way to quiet down the SNS (our "Arghhh" nervous system) is to engage the second part of the ANS—the parasympathetic nervous system (pSNS) or the "rest and digest," "Ahhhh" nervous system). While easy to do in practice, it's hard to do when your brain is in freak-out mode.

Sympathetic Nervous System (SNS) versus Parasympathetic Nervous System (pSNS) Characteristics

SNS	pSNS
Fight, Flight	Calm, Aware (or Freeze)
Cortisol, Adrenaline	Serotonin, Dopamine
Tunnel vision/ Narrow thinking	Creative problem-solving
Irrational decision-making	Logical decision-making
Impulsive, Reactive	Able to inhibit behaviors and respond mindfully
Immune suppression, weight gain, autoimmune disorders	Healthy blood vessels, functioning immune system, weight moderation

It's crucial that we find ways to calm the SNS. Left unchecked, the best-case scenario is that we become overweight, distracted, impatient, snarky, and unproductive. Worst case is severe health problems including obesity, diabetes, high blood pressure, and heart attack.

The vagus nerve—which travels from our heads (helping us communicate and understand others' emotions through facial expressions) down to our hearts and lungs, and continuing to the stomach, where our very real "gut impulses" originate—regulates this tug of war between the SNS and pSNS. When operating well, good vagal tone keeps us from going into fight-or-flight (SNS) or freeze (the extreme place the pSNS can take us). Good vagal tone also helps us respond mindfully, instead of reacting impulsively. A strong ANS also helps us develop what many of my clients refer to as "executive presence," enabling us to act in ways that make us more influential and help us earn others' respect and trust. While our brains and bodies aren't well-suited to today's frenetic world, it's possible to thrive by adopting a few new habits. Throughout this book, you'll find many ways to quiet the SNS so you can take charge of your reactions and be your best, most at ease, self. I know your time is precious, so many of these tips take an instant or a few minutes to work. Regardless of your current stress level, there are tools inside this book to help you clear the muck that's snuffing out your brilliant spark.

> *As far as we can discern, the sole purpose of human existence is to kindle a light in the darkness of mere being.*
>
> —CARL JUNG

Let's take a break from burnout and see what brilliance looks like.

Brilliance

I first met Lola over two decades ago when we both worked at Oracle Corporation. We were both very young and very outside our elements: I was a French major teaching attorneys contract licensing, and she was one of my students. Lola was striking: lovely and elegant, bearing an accent cultivated in Nigeria and London—but she wasn't yet living a brilliant life. Lola would go on to attain senior positions at other high-tech Silicon Valley firms until one day, her boss walked into her office, tears streaming down her face, with this message: "There's been a restructure and you're affected. Today's your last day." After the shock wore off, Lola realized what a gift she'd been given. While she loved the people she worked with, she didn't love the work or the grueling commute. She now had complete freedom, and a severance salary for twelve months. She was offered a contract position at salesforce.com ten days later, and now had two paychecks coming in. She could have coasted in "cubicle nation" (Pam Slim's brilliant label for the corporate world), amassing more stock options and padding her savings, but she was on the blah side of the stress curve: not quite burned out, but bored and restless, for inside Lola was an artist. She began taking classes in jewelry making and confirmed that this was her passion. She reinvented herself as Lola Fenhirst, and her stunning work has been featured in *Forbes*. Recently, her pieces were worn at Fashion Week in New York. She now shines as brilliantly as her artistry.

You don't have to quit your job and become an artist to become brilliant. One of my former clients started her career as a musician and earned modest success as an opening act for a famous band on their world tour. But she and her musician husband wanted more stability so they could start a family. She left music and entered corporate life, where she found a role in which she used her strengths every day in a field that improves lives.

Plus, even if you have an artist inside you, quitting your day job won't necessarily lead to brilliance. In fact, it may cause you tremendous stress. It's extremely hard to make a living by creating, and you can't live a brilliant life if you can't pay the bills. Elizabeth Gilbert makes this case beautifully in her book *Big Magic*, where she urges us to never burden our creativity with the need to earn a living, but to find work that meets practical needs while you create on the side, as my friend Lola did to fund her luxury jewelry business. While finding your vocation is a noble quest, this book ain't about that. If that's your goal, check out Martha Beck's *Finding Your Own North Star*, Pamela Slim's *Escape from Cubicle Nation* or *Body of Work*, or Tara Mohr's *Playing Big*. This book is about being the best you can be right now, making the most of your mental state, physical health, relationships, and environment.

FORGET ABOUT WORK-LIFE BALANCE

When I ask all my new clients what they most want to achieve during our work together, nearly everyone names "work–life balance." Then I ask what balance looks like to them. Usually, it involves less time at the office, and more quality time with self, friends, and family. When I dig deeper, I always discover that they really want something much more than balance. The more they get in touch with their own fears, emotions, values, and heart's desires, the farther off course they feel.

I met Samantha in my leadership workshop, "Conversations for Brilliance." I could tell she was an inspiring, wicked-smart leader with that coveted combination of emotional intelligence, expertise, and work ethic. After the workshop she asked if I'd be her personal coach, saying that she wanted better work–life balance—more free time, more energy to work out, and more quality time with her young daughter and husband. She also wanted to feel less stress from her grueling job and commute. Samantha described herself as a people-pleaser. She'd been the peacemaker in her family growing up. This identity carried over in her work life. Her can-do attitude, coupled with resourcefulness, expertise, and a talented team, helped her become a dumping zone for troubled projects, as well as an incubator for bringing nascent ideas to thriving life.

This role had a cost.

She was exhausted, depleted, and deflated, feeling like she was taking more and more on for little personal and professional gain. She was constantly tired and was frustrated that she couldn't lose her pregnancy weight, despite eating well. After a couple of intake sessions, it became clear that our work would involve helping her draw stronger boundaries and use more declarative language at home and work. I also urged her to see a holistic medical doctor who would run a bazillion blood tests to find the underlying imbalance that was resulting in fatigue and weight gain.

At the end of our program, she gave me one of the best compliments I could ever receive when she said, "Thanks to you, I have my mojo back." To her, "mojo" meant a sense of power, strength, and integration. A feeling that she could make life happen, instead of having life happen to her. A feeling of being energized versus depleted.

Samantha's story is unique, just as yours is. But the underlying desire to thrive is universal. As you may have experienced, striving for so-called balance—just the right amount of hours spent at home and work—usually leads to frustration and guilt. So, let's set aside notions about work–life balance and play a bigger (yet, ironically, more achievable) game. I suggest we aim for Whole-Life Integration.

My new executive clients are sometimes surprised when I ask them about sleep, diet, family, friends, and fun. I tell them my goal is to help them be their best selves, and to do that, I have to focus on the whole person. Many clients are more than ready to have these conversations. Evan, a vice president of operations at a global wine company, hired me to help him be a stronger leader. For years, we had a great partnership helping him communicate strategy, lead through change, and engage with his team. But he quickly grasped the personal potential within a coaching partnership. He came to recognize the voice inside his head that told him he "wasn't good enough" and "wasn't doing enough." It's a voice we all have, and one that can cause us great pain. Evan learned to see it for what it was and practice gratitude for all that he had and had created. He began to trust himself and allow praise from his loyal team members to actually land. He stopped saying yes to every activity that came across his path, and learned to deeply value simple walks and routines with his loving family. He partnered with my holistic MD, Morgan Camp, and lost about thirty pounds, gained energy, and improved his sleep.

My one-word term for Whole-Life Integration is *brilliance.* Brilliance happens when we feel a sense of freedom and agency over our lives: ease, instead of struggle; freedom, instead of being trapped in a toxic body, relationship, thought pattern, or job. Brilliance is the opposite of burned out, and a serious upgrade from blah. It's about reigniting that spark in all of us that has dimmed over the years. It's about integrating and strengthening all aspects of our lives so we feel like we're capable of stepping into our glorious, radiant potential.

Brilliance may seem impossible but it's not. You were born with a spark, and then life piled on. This book is about how to clear the muck so you can shine brilliantly again.

We all know people who are very strong in one aspect of their lives, yet weak in another. A person who has incredible financial success but poor relationships and high stress, for example, is not leading his most brilliant life. A leader with a great mind for strategy but little empathy for others won't be able to truly develop a loyal, world-class team.

The Four Realms of Brilliance

We experience brilliance when all aspects of our lives are integrated—*inner and outer worlds*—as well as our relationship to *self and others*. My teacher James Flaherty, founder of New Ventures West integral coaching school, is one of the inspirations for this model.

**Whole Life Integration
(Brilliance)**

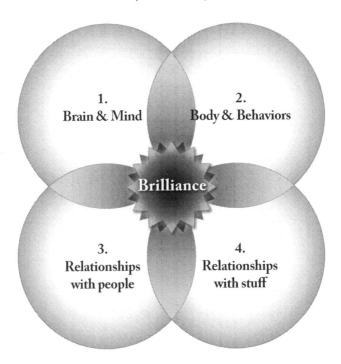

1. BRAIN AND MIND

This is the realm of the conversations we have with ourselves—our thoughts and beliefs—and the effects of those conversations inside our bodies—our moods, emotions, and stress level. This realm becomes brilliant when our thoughts and beliefs drive us to take actions that align with our highest visions and values. We know our inner world is brilliant when we feel a sense of ease, gratitude, and emotional flow versus stagnation.

2. BODY AND BEHAVIORS

This is the outward manifestation of our inner world. How do we behave? Do we honk the horn at people trying to merge in rush hour or let them in? What does our body look like? Brilliant or blob? What does our speech sound like? Judgmental or curious? Stressed or calm? Weak or confident? We know this element is brilliant when we feel strong, grounded, healthy, energized, rested, and productive.

3. RELATIONSHIPS WITH PEOPLE

This is about how we connect with others. This element becomes brilliant when we have high-quality relationships full of ease, trust, love, empathy, and curiosity. When we have strong boundaries and limit our time with those people who exude toxic energy. This element glows brightest when we're surrounded by people who help us be our best selves.

4. RELATIONSHIPS WITH STUFF

This realm includes our surroundings, possessions, time, and technology. How does your work and home environment feel? Is it organized, beautiful, peaceful and supportive? Or is it cluttered with distractions including piles of papers, unfolded laundry, blaring TV, dirty dishes, drab décor, messy closets, and "pinging" devices alerting you about non-urgent incoming emails and notifications? We maximize the potential in this realm when we eliminate clutter and increase beauty around us, design our days to help us fulfill our mission on earth, have ample financial security, and use technology wisely and mindfully to achieve our goals and connect with others. We use our time intentionally so that our accomplishments are aligned with our values and goals.

Sounds great, right? Who wouldn't want this kind of integration? But it may seem daunting and even impossible. I know what it's like to feel out of balance—or *dis-integrated*. When I was twenty-two and broke my body in a car accident, I gave up on my potential. I felt trapped in a body and life that seemed doomed. But gradually, I gathered support and searched for a way to come back. It's constant work—more than two decades later, I'm still in a healing appointment at least once weekly—but it's worth it to be strong enough to live a life that's aligned with who I want to be.

And that's the thing about brilliance: it's not a destination you reach and then set up camp. It's more like a journey with unpredictable twists and turns. It's easy to fall off the path, but with attention and shifting, you can find your way back again. Through my own experience and through working with my clients, I know that anyone can become brilliantly integrated. And while it won't happen overnight, a powerful shift can happen in an instant. It's the shift where you see a light under the door of whatever prison of the soul you find yourself trapped in. Where you start to believe that not only is a change possible, but that it *must* happen. You don't have to know how to change in order to feel this shift. You just have to believe that it's possible.

WHERE TO BEGIN?

It's not realistic to work on all four realms at once because the brain hates massive change. (We'll talk about why, and how to overcome this in the next section.) One way we trick the brain is by choosing only one thing to work on at a time, and by starting small.

But how to choose where to begin? Here's a preview of what's to come:

1. We'll dive deeper into each of the four realms of brilliance, so you'll get a sense of what a truly brilliant life could look like.

2. You'll take the six-minute Brilliant Life Assessment I give to my coaching clients. This will give you a clear visual of where you're most and least integrated.

3. Then you'll choose *one* area that you want to improve. It should be an area that's causing you so much pain that you're motivated to improve. As you read through the book, you'll think about and work with this chosen focus area.

4. You'll learn how to change any habit—including sleeping better—and along the way I'll provide tools to help you make positive shifts.

Now is your time to ignite the spark inside you. It may be buried under a pile of dust and accrued odds and ends, but trust me, it's there.

---

*Every block of stone has a statue inside it
and it is the task of the sculptor to discover it.*

—MICHELANGELO BUONARROTI

CHAPTER TWO:

Tame Your Thoughts

*I've got 99 problems and 86 of them
are completely made up scenarios in my head.*

—UNKNOWN

When I first met Stacey—an intelligent, successful, high-performing leader—she was consumed with painful emotions. She'd just returned from Canada where she had had to fire a valuable, trusted employee because he committed fraud. Rather than do a typical, first meeting, get-to-know-each-other session, we dealt directly with her overwhelming feelings. I asked Stacey what thought caused her the most pain. She said, "I'm most upset that he betrayed me." She ruminated over this, dumping toxic stress-related chemicals into her body. (We'll get to how I helped Stacey free herself from this painful thought in a moment.)

Stacey was experiencing an all-too-common breakdown in Realm One of the Brilliance Model: her inner world was in turmoil. As a reminder from the last chapter, this is the realm of our brain and mind, and the conversations we have with ourselves—our thoughts, beliefs, moods, emotions, and stress level. Regardless of how smart, talented, healthy, or wealthy you are, you cannot live brilliantly until you learn to manage your thoughts and emotions.

All of us have found ourselves in Stacey's position, with a painful thought we just can't seem to shake. Maybe someone cut you off in traffic and it bugged you the whole commute. Or maybe the company issued yet another dictum that had you steaming all day. Or maybe you keep running a frustrating conversation over and over again in your mind. Maybe you held it together during work and then dumped accumulated frustration on the closest innocent victim . . . and later felt really, really crappy about it.

I'm giving you permission to drop the guilt about any unfortunate emotional outbursts—and I'll give you tools for preventing future ones. Unless you're a Buddhist monk who practices compassion meditation for hours a day, outbursts are almost inevitable because, sadly, we're wired to ruminate on negative—not positive—thoughts. Our brains have five times as many circuits for negative thinking than positive—another unfortunate survival trait that hasn't been upgraded to fit modern times.

The brain is like Velcro for negative experiences but Teflon for positive ones.
—Rick Hanson, PhD

Your brain is a master storyteller. Its job is to make sense of moment-by-moment inputs. And since it never has all the data it needs, it fills in the gaps, weaving so seamlessly that the story in our head feels like the inescapable *truth.*

The cell grouping that comprises this storyteller part of our brain is about the size of a peanut, and it does its job so well, we ride along as if we had no choice, letting it loop and continually flood our bodies with cortisol and other stress-related chemicals. *Story becomes truth.*

Getting hooked on emotionally charged narratives of anger, resentment, guilt, shame, or fear for long periods can have devastating consequences for our physical and mental well-being, because of the powerful ways they affect our emotional and physiological circuitry. It's vital to our health and relationships that we learn how to experience the emotion and then shift away. And if you're in a leadership role (at work or home), it's vital to the mental and physical health of everyone around you because a leader's (or parent's) mood is contagious.

Emotions Call the Shots

My clients like to think of themselves as reasonable people who make decisions based on data and information. It's my job to tell them—and you— that's not how it works: our emotions (particularly if left unrecognized) determine our actions, which then determine our results. This used to be a hard sell in my coaching engagements and workshops. Some people don't like talking about emotions and they *really* don't like feeling them. I had one leader tell me, "Emotions have

Although many of us may think of ourselves as thinking creatures that feel, biologically we are feeling creatures that think.

—Jill Bolte Taylor

no place in the workplace." I wondered aloud, "So, where do you put them?" It turns out she was like a volcano—peaceful and calm until, on rare occasions, she'd erupt with surprisingly strong reactions.

We hire people for their skills, but the whole person shows up.
—Chester Barnard

We don't include our emotions on our résumé. You won't see: "When I'm under pressure, I get angry," or "When I make a mistake, I blame others to deflect attention away from me," or "When I don't get my way, I'm a jackass"; but our ability to regulate our emotions will determine our success far more than our work experience or expertise.

Don't just take my word for it. The 2002 Nobel Prize in Economics went to Daniel Kahneman, who proved that people make economic decisions first emotionally (limbic/lizard brain) and then logically (prefrontal cortex). Of course, you probably already knew that our relationship to money is emotional: anyone who observes the stock market knows that it's anything but rational. And you probably feel more hesitation when you pay for something with cash rather than a credit card. Many of our purchases fulfill emotional needs, and we back them up with logic. I don't *need* an Italian crafted handbag, I can fit all my stuff in a recycled tote bag. No one *needs* a Tesla when you can buy a perfectly nice Prius. Fortunately for the global market, emotions often overrule logic.

When we fail to recognize our emotions, they grow into moods that leave us feeling trapped under a great weight: sadness becomes depression; anger mutates to rage and resentment; happiness morphs into an escape from reality. We need to listen to our emotions and act accordingly: sadness may indicate we need to grieve something we've lost; anger tells us we need to protect ourselves and establish boundaries; fear tells us to be wary because something we care about is threatened; and love tells us to be deeply appreciative and savor.

In Stacey's case, she was experiencing anger, disappointment, and betrayal. Those emotions created a story that this employee somehow intended to betray her. As a result, she experienced shortness of breath, chest and stomach pain, and headaches. Her adrenals were dumping cortisol into her system and elevating her stress. Clearly, she wasn't her best self. If she didn't quiet the story, she'd experience more harmful consequences, among them dumping her horrific mood on innocent employees.

Recently, a client told me that his wife nearly died during childbirth twenty years ago. At the time, he was in graduate school, working full-time with the only household income, with two new babies and a very sick wife. He went into crisis management mode and took action to get through that time, ignoring any emotions and becoming oblivious to his feelings. Then, years later, he had a panic attack so severe he thought he was dying of a heart attack. Nothing was seriously wrong with him. The emotions were just finding their own way out—painfully. His time in the ER was his wake-up call. He wasn't superhuman, and he needed to take better care of his own physical and emotional needs. Only then did he learn to honor his emotions and make an effort to reduce stress.

My clients invariably begin our coaching conversations by telling me about something that happened; they focus on who did what, and what happened as a result. I'll ask them what emotions they felt before they took the action. Then I ask what emotions and thoughts could have motivated the other person to take such action. I ask because *results don't just happen*: our emotions fuel the thoughts that prompt decisions and actions that *then* produce results.

As Susan Scott wrote in *Fierce Conversations*, those results happen gradually, then suddenly, as in: "Suddenly, my pants don't fit," or "Suddenly, my credit card is maxed out," or "Suddenly, my best employee quit and went to the competition," or "Suddenly, my spouse left me."

THOUGHTS

We think almost constantly (over forty thousand thoughts a day), *yet we rarely think about our thoughts*. Instead, we go through life on autopilot, letting our thoughts direct us, instead of directing our thoughts so that they align with our values and goals. We also fail to notice how incorrect (and often toxic) our thoughts really are. Because our brain cares more about preserving our energy instead of accuracy (in case we need to flee a charging lion), we constantly make cognitive errors that we steadfastly believe are correct. When a thought is powerful enough, we upgrade it to a belief—a thought we decide is true— regardless of contradicting evidence. In Stacey's case, she absolutely believed that this employee intended to betray her. And that led to an even more potentially harmful belief: "I was stupid to trust him, and would be stupid to trust others in the future."

ACTIONS

When we fail to recognize and manage our emotions and thoughts, they can prompt us to act in regrettable ways: snap at our child, raise our voice in a meeting, blabber incoherently in a high-stakes presentation, or show our cards too early in a negotiation. We have around three-hundredths of a second between the time when our brain feels an emotion, then produces a thought, and our mouth opens. Anyone who's ever said anything regrettable, or sent an e-mail by accident, knows just how hard it is to catch that window and redirect your actions.

Luckily, we have a self-regulation system in the brain that acts like a pair of brakes. Left unattended, it will wear down, just like your car's brakes. Hunger, emotional and physical pain, exhaustion, and stress all weaken the brakes. But with effort, we can strengthen them. When self-regulation is high, we can create a pause before we speak or act, then decide what action best fits the situation. Your reputation, relationships, and results depend on you developing the ability to respond instead of react.

Without awareness and self-regulation, our actions are on autopilot; we're actors in our lives, playing out a familiar role.

The work of leadership demands that you manage not only the critical adaptive responses within and surrounding your business but also your own thinking and emotions.

—Ronald Heifetz,
senior lecturer at Harvard
Kennedy School

We get so immersed in the show called *life* that we forget we own the script rights. We become lost in our character, allowing emotions and circumstances to direct us. If you want to take control of your results and your life, get off the stage, get out of character, and get into the director's chair.

Some people don't want to learn to self-regulate. They claim, "I am who I am and they need to get used to it," or, "I say it like it is, and if they don't like it, tough," or, "I'm too old to change." Those people don't tend to hire coaches or, if they do, they ignore the coach's advice. Your ability to connect with and influence others depends upon your ability to appropriately adapt your thoughts, beliefs, and behaviors. This is much harder work than remaining stuck in your personality pattern (and blaming others for your poor results), but it's worth it.

Without a director you are a mere automaton, driven by greed, fear, or habit.

—David Rock,
Your Brain at Work

Later in the book, you'll learn how to efficiently change habits, including your habitual thoughts and responses.

RESULTS

You could live your life (as most people do) as though things happen to you and you have no control over the results. This belief will put you squarely in the role of victim, leaving you powerless to improve your state and your results. Your brain loves victim mode because you're off the hook when it comes to changing. You can just coast, and blame external circumstances for your subpar results.

You can tell you're in victim mode by observing how you make excuses, complain, and justify your results. Let's say you arrive late to a meeting. Do you blame the traffic ("There was an accident")? Or, do you take responsibility for the fact that you failed to leave early enough? One of them you can change, and one of them you cannot. If you want to live a brilliant life, you must take on the belief that results happen *because of the actions you take*.

I once had the challenge of working under a senior vice president whose actions led to widespread fear and poor morale. Her habits included poor listening, distrust (she'd only listen to a few people in her inner circle, who she brought with her to every new job), intolerance for differing opinions, making ungrounded assumptions, and exerting high control. While she may have attained executive status, she never lasted long in a company. Eventually, she was walked out of the building by security (for ethical infractions) two years into her toxic reign. She had to leave the Bay Area because too many bridges were burned. She didn't *want* to be ineffective—no one does. But she hadn't done the work to heal whatever emotional wounds she'd incurred in the past, and to learn emotional intelligence, which involves self-awareness, empathy, trust, and authentically adapting to people and situations.

~*A personal story*~

It was December 1992 and I was a senior at Arizona State University. Midterm exams were over, and I was driving to work, eager to earn money to help fund my final semester. I was set to travel home to Kansas in two days. Like most people, I was in a rush, when suddenly, I was involved in a multi-car crash.

Let's trace my path to results.

Believe it or not, the first emotion I recall feeling after the crash was anxiety about being late to work. Next, anxiety about health insurance: was the ambulance ride covered or would my parents get hit with a huge bill? I'd never had a major injury and took good health for granted. I was also in shock and didn't even notice my bodily sensations. I time traveled away from my current state to worry about a future state.

I also felt fear. Specifically, I feared that I wouldn't be able to go to work and earn money. (Can you tell I was a little Type A and disconnected from my body?) Those emotions led to these thoughts that would shape things to come: I must find a doctor fast; all doctors are the same; my mom (who had a back injury) has a doctor, so I'll just save time and go to him.

Beliefs are thoughts we decide to make true.

—Sean Stephenson, *Get Off Your "But"*

And that's what I did. I booked an appointment with my mom's doctor, even though he hadn't helped her much, and was under investigation for supposedly performing unnecessary surgeries. Smart, huh?

Years later, I learned a very important lesson that I hope you learn faster: doctors have different beliefs about health and treatment. If you want to be healed, you better learn what your doctor believes, and if his beliefs don't include healing you, find someone else.

My doctor believed that I was irreversibly crippled. And I believed him.

Given that belief, what treatment do you think he recommended for me? He said I should stop physical therapy (it wouldn't help), take pain medicine, and accept the fact that I might not be able to work again. As a reminder, I was twenty-three, about to graduate summa cum laude, and here I have an expert telling me to not even bother trying to hold down a job. What do you think my results were?

I got worse.

I became depressed.

I spent my limited energy blaming the man who rear-ended me.

In victim mode, I had little chance of escaping my self-inflicted mental trap. I graduated, moved to the Bay Area, and one day, desperate with pain and having no local doctor, checked myself into the Stanford Hospital emergency room. There, a nurse recommended I see Robert Gamburd, doctor to the San Francisco 49ers football team. What do you think his context about injuries was? He believed he'd seen worse and helped them get better, so he could help me, and he could get me back in the game if he patiently assessed and figured out exactly what was wrong with me.

How do you think these beliefs shaped his actions with regard to my treatment? He asked a lot of questions, ran many tests, and examined my movements carefully. Then he recommended a blend of treatments including steroid shots, high dosages of ibuprofen, physical therapy, Rolfing, a chiropractor, and eventually, a minimally invasive surgery that melted the scar tissue in the core of a spinal disk. What were my results? I can now sit, drive, exercise, work, and lead a full life.

But there was also a surprising and troubling result. About a year into treatment, I developed rheumatoid arthritis. I had a hunch that all the steroids in my system may have triggered the autoimmune disorder. I ran this theory by Dr. Gamburd. Because of his open-mindedness (a trait I find is rare in many medical specialists), he thought I could be right, and he knew a doctor who could help. I stopped seeing the rheumatologist and went to Dr. Raj Patel in Redwood City, California. That was perhaps the best decision I've ever made.

Dr. Patel's context about health is that disease results from an imbalance, and that many diseases can be cured if you find and fix the imbalance. He referred me to a Nambudripad's Allergy Elimination Techniques (NAET) practitioner, and twenty-four hours after being treated for gluten intolerance, my rheumatoid arthritis symptoms went away. That was in 1998. (You can find a NAET practitioner at NAET.com. Choose one who is highly certified.)

That was the beginning of a dramatic shift in my context about health. My new belief is: if I get injured or ill, I'll find a way to fix it. While that might not sound realistic, it's worked well for me so far. Almost two decades later, Dr. Patel is helping me overcome Lyme disease and mold poisoning. It's been a slow process, but three years after diagnosis, I'm ninety percent better than I was, and I'm on a relentless quest to get back to feeling even better than before I contracted Lyme.

Overcoming Harmful Beliefs

While tragedies often cause people to reappraise long-held beliefs, you don't have to wait for something bad to happen to shift your context; you can alter your life's trajectory now. You can assess your beliefs and upgrade those that aren't getting you the results you want. I borrow the word "upgrade" in this context from Victoria Castle, author of *The Trance of Scarcity.*

Anyone who's flown commercial knows what it feels like to walk through the first-class cabin and then squeeze into your economy seat. In economy, the ride will be uncomfortable and you'll arrive stiff and tired. Upgraded, you're still on the same plane (in this case, your life) but with more ease, able to act differently on arrival.

> *If you're going to live your life based on delusions (and you are, because we all do), then why not at least select a delusion that is helpful?*
>
> —ELIZABETH GILBERT,
> *Big Magic*

One core harmful belief that haunts us all is some variation of "I'm not good enough," which leads to any number of actions, including:

- I say yes too often, because I want to prove my worthiness.
- I give up trying because I'll never be good enough.
- I don't take risks (like writing a book, or starting a company) because I fear that I'm not able to do what needs to be done.
- I don't speak up in meetings.
- I use self-deprecating language that makes me less influential.
- I get easily intimidated around others and appear weak and unconvincing.
- I numb myself with food, drugs, or alcohol.

If you're thinking to yourself that any part of what I'm suggesting is unrealistic; that you can't change your circumstances just by shifting your thoughts, well . . . you have a point. I'm not suggesting you have a magic wand and can create anything just by thinking about it. There will be unavoidable storms; there will be times when you can't fix something because it's outside your control. And, as you probably know all too well, you can't change other people, no matter how hard you may try. At best, you can only influence them to change themselves. But you are not powerless; No matter what reality hits you, *you can choose your reaction*. And that choice will affect your state, your decisions, your actions, and eventually, your outcomes.

Remember my brilliant friend Lola? On a recent hike, Lola said to me, "Even when I couldn't pay my debts to gem dealers and my bank account was getting dangerously low, I knew in my heart that I'd be a successful, global brand." Lola believed, as Jack Canfield espouses, that the universe is out to help her. As such, she didn't give up when things got bad. She took a lucrative contract job as corporate counsel to help fund her dream. She put herself in situations that connected her to a great PR team, and she kept moving forward, undeterred by setbacks.

The last of the human freedoms —to choose one's attitude in any given set of circumstances.

—Viktor Frankl

A sense of freedom awaits you. Freedom from relentless fear, anger, guilt, and regret: freedom from the hole your thoughts have dug for you.

Even when we know we have a painful, debilitating thought, and we want to change it, doing so can be tough. It's as if our brain is stuck like a broken vinyl record, replaying the same thought despite our realization that it's harming our state and results. So, let's shift from theory to action, and change your life for the better with a simple process I use with every client who's ready to shift away from a painful thought.

Your Six-Step Thought Upgrade Tool

As you read further, you have two choices: you can read about this process just to gain information, or you can actually get relief by working with a negative thought that's haunting you.

1

STEP ONE: Name the story/thought/belief. What does your debilitating, limiting story sound like? Warning: this is not a fun step for most of us. If you're not ready to dig deep and don't have a trusted partner to help you upgrade your *core* limiting belief, you can work with any belief that's causing you pain. For example, perhaps you're upset with a colleague at work, or someone at home, and your belief is "He doesn't do his fair share." Let go of any self-judgment during these steps and take on a neutral observer mindset.

Tip: If you're not sure what thought to work with first, brainstorm a list of negative thoughts you've had recently, and pick one that you'd like to upgrade.

Write your painful thought here:

_____

_____

_____

_____

_____

_____

_____

_____

_____

STEP TWO: Ask, yourself, "What am I likely to do—or not do—as a result of that belief?" For example, let's say your core belief is "I don't trust my employee to do the work as well as I do." Your actions may include *withholding work* that could help her stretch and be more engaged at work. Or, if we refer back to the example thought in Step One, if you think someone else isn't pulling their fair share of the workload, you might *speak to them in a resentful tone, or speak negatively about them to others.*

What action or inaction is your negative thought producing or likely to produce? Write it below:

_____

_____

_____

_____

_____

_____

_____

_____

_____

_____

_____

_____

_____

3

STEP THREE: Ask yourself, "What results does it get me physically, emotionally, and in relationships?" Using the prior example about failing to delegate work, *your employee gets bored, disengaged, and resentful, while your pile of work keeps growing, and you don't have enough capacity to do it all. You work late into the night on things you could have delegated, producing exhaustion, tension, and possibly resentment in your family, and a feeling of guilt for working too much.*

What results are your actions (or inactions) producing or likely to produce? Write them below:

_____

_____

_____

_____

_____

_____

_____

_____

_____

_____

_____

_____

STEP FOUR: Upgrade the painful, debilitating thought.
In this step, you're looking for a plausible replacement to the painful thought. Brainstorm possible new stories by asking yourself or a neutral party, "How else can I look at this?" You know you've got a good upgrade when it produces these factors: *You believe it; it brings relief when you think it; and it motivates new, improved behaviors.* This step is best done with an objective partner who can toss out ideas and not worry about how many you shoot down. Your upgrade might sound like "If I delegate meaningful work, and support her until she's confident and competent, she'll be happier and I'll have more time to work on things I've been neglecting."

Note: an upgrade is not a flip. You can't just reverse a thought and expect your brain to believe it. For example, if your painful thought is that he doesn't do his fair share, you can't just tell yourself, "He does enough" and expect your brain to believe it. Your upgrade might sound instead like, "Something must be getting in the way of him doing more. Perhaps it's the way I communicate the importance of my requests, or perhaps he has responsibilities I'm not aware of."

Select an upgraded thought/belief and write it below:

_____

_____

_____

_____

_____

_____

5

STEP FIVE: Predict what new, improved actions and results this new belief is likely to produce. Then begin taking those actions, one baby step at a time.

What actions will this upgraded thought likely produce? Write them below:

_____

_____

_____

_____

_____

_____

_____

_____

_____

_____

_____

_____

_____

_____

_____

_____

_____

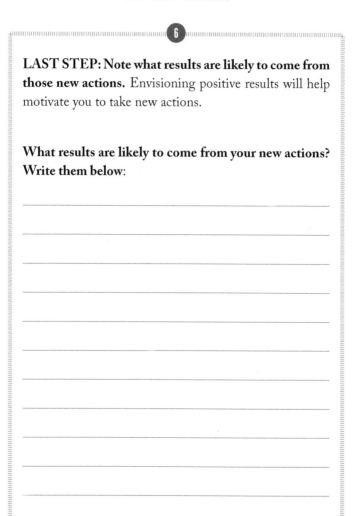

6

LAST STEP: Note what results are likely to come from those new actions. Envisioning positive results will help motivate you to take new actions.

What results are likely to come from your new actions? Write them below:

_____

_____

_____

_____

_____

_____

_____

_____

_____

_____

_____

_____

You can grab my Thought Upgrade Template
from my website:
www.BrillianceInc.com/Resources

HOW TO MAKE IT STICK

Your old, painful thought won't disappear overnight. It's become a habit, and as such, your brain has created abundant neural connections enforcing it. You can supplant it by repeating the new thought many times daily until it becomes a stronger belief. Notice when you think the original painful thought. Catch yourself thinking it, and replace it with the reappraisal. *Act whenever possible from the reappraisal.* You could think the new thought every time that person writes or speaks to you. But any cue will work. For example, think the upgraded thought every time you take a sip of water, or open your e-mail, or touch a door handle.

> *If I want to retain my inner peace, I must be willing to consistently and persistently tend the garden of my mind moment by moment . . .*
>
> —Jill Bolte Taylor

THE THOUGHT UPGRADE TOOL IN ACTION

I once had the pleasure of helping an amazing woman upgrade her core identity story. She led a team in the World Trade Center, and on Sept 11, 2001, she was too sick to go to work.

Her entire team perished.

She suffered deeply from grief and survivor's guilt. Her running story was: "I should have been there; I don't deserve to be alive." She wanted to be free of this story that felt so true and inescapable. So we started brainstorming and I tossed phrase after phrase out at her. When I said, "You are a conduit for God's grace," she stopped me, took a deep breath in, and let out a deep exhale. As she was a devout Christian, this phrase landed. She could believe it because it meant she had work to do. It wasn't about her. It wasn't about deserving. It was about helping others. And she couldn't do that unless she was alive.

More recently, I worked with a new leader who told me he'd always suffered from low confidence. I asked him if others told him he was hard on himself and he said, "All the time." In fact, his boss sings his praises regularly. So, I asked him, "How well is this story—that you aren't as good as others—working out for you?" "Not so good," he said.

I gave him a very slight upgrade to consider—one I thought his brain could accept: "Being hard on myself isn't helping." It was still negative, but it was a good baby step in the right direction. The following week, after he'd been repeating that belief, taking a more confident body posture, and using two apps to help increase positivity and calmness, he was ready for another upgrade.

I asked him what actions his "I don't measure up" story was producing. He told me that he often compared himself to a colleague who was great at speaking off-the-cuff and telling stories. As a result of this comparison, my client would become quiet in meetings, rarely speaking up because he didn't feel adequate. He'd also take on a small, stooped body posture in his chair, attempting to avoid drawing any attention. I asked him to name something he was better at than his eloquent colleague. Without hesitation, he said, "Managing people." My client said that he'd heard many complaints from his direct reports about his colleague's leadership style. Meanwhile, my client's direct reports love working for him. So, I offered this upgrade: "I bring unique gifts to my work." He immediately felt a shift. He didn't have to put this person on a pedestal anymore. He was able to see that he didn't have to envy his peer's presentation skills: he could admire those skills and learn from him. This new story freed him from his constant and painful comparing habit. His job now is to repeat the story over and over until it becomes an embedded belief.

Remember Stacey's painful story from the beginning of the chapter—that her trusted employee had betrayed her? In our first meeting, I quickly sketched out the Thought Upgrade Tool, which helped visually distract her from her story and gave her a sense that there was a process that would bring her relief. I asked Stacey what sensations she felt in her body when she had this thought. That question shifted her attention and paused the looping thought. Then I asked what actions this thought was prompting and what results might yield from those actions. Just considering that question brought up anxiety when she realized that she'd be less trusting of everyone, and that would eventually damage her ability to have strong relationships or be an effective leader.

Then I asked her to look at the story from another angle: to put herself in his shoes. How likely was it that his actions were motivated by an intent to betray her? And what might he likely be thinking and feeling right now? She sat back in her chair and said, "Shit, this isn't about me at all. I wouldn't want to be in his shoes for anything. He has to be consumed with shame and regret about his actions, and for letting me and his family down, not to mention fear about his future." She took a deep breath and felt freed. It's not always that easy to untangle painful thoughts. But it helps when you catch them early. She'd stepped off the stage and become the director, shifting the story from one where she was the victim of treacherous betrayal, to one where she was witness to a dear friend's self-destructive behavior.

REFLECTION QUESTION

When will you repeat your new upgraded thought so that it becomes embedded as a stronger belief than the old toxic belief? Designate cues that are easy to remember (washing hands, walking through a doorway, thinking about the old thought, touching a doorknob, etc.).

CHAPTER THREE:

Reinvent Your Outer Self

*As soon as one sees another person, an impression
is formed. This happens so quickly—just a
small fraction of a second—that what we see
can sometimes dominate what we know.*

—NICHOLAS RULE, University of Toronto

Tom has been a humble, loyal employee of the same
company for more than two decades. He began as a
college intern, and through his knowledge, talent, can-do
attitude, and likability, rose through the ranks to lead a
large technology team. When I met him, he had a new
boss who believed that he was capable of even greater
influence. His boss asked him to become less of a manager
and more of a strategic leader, shaping hospital patient
care for the better through technology. Tom would have
to work less with his team and more with top leaders
in the medical industry. This would be tough; Tom felt
authentically confident working with his team and peers,
but when it came to meetings on the twenty-eighth

floor, where all the "important executives" worked, Tom's confidence plummeted and he felt like more like an intern than vice president.

Tom made two small but significant changes to his appearance. First, he studied facial expressions and learned what his own facial muscles did when he felt annoyed or frustrated. He learned to moderate his facial response and remain more neutral (he adopted a "poker face"). This actually helped him feel calmer inside and find a pause so he could ask an open-ended question like "Can you say more about that?" or "What concerns you most about that?" He also started wearing suits, which helped him feel more confident. He started to feel more like a peer or professional consultant to the leaders who once intimidated him. He stood and sat more confidently, which created a Superman effect on his Clark Kent persona.

The previous chapter examined our inner world—our thoughts, sensations, and emotions. In this chapter, we'll discuss our external self—all observable physical traits and behaviors: what and how you present to the world. In the last chapter, we learned how our emotions prompt thoughts that affect our physical state and motivate actions that shape our results (for better or worse). In this section, we'll see how it works both ways: when you change your outward state, you can positively affect your emotions and thoughts, and prompt behaviors that will produce better results.

Amy Cuddy's TED talk about body language and confidence had over thirty-six million views as of writing this chapter. In it she discusses her Harvard research proving that people who held a big posture for just two minutes lowered their cortisol (stress hormone) and increased testosterone (confidence hormone) levels. So, next time you need a boost of calm confidence, stand tall with feet apart, hands at hips like Wonder Woman or Superman (imaginary cape flying behind you in the breeze). While Cuddy's research shows that changing your physical state almost instantly changes your emotional and mental state, long-term change happens over time, through repetition. Recall Susan Scott's observation (inspired by Hemingway) that results happen gradually, then suddenly. I sometimes joke that elves entered my closet and moved the buttons on my pants, so that they no longer fit. But the truth is that I made and acted on many decisions (French fries, anyone?) that led to that moment.

This chapter is about aligning our outward appearance and actions with who and how we want to be in the world.

The Importance of First Impressions

First impressions are more heavily influenced by nonverbal cues than verbal cues. A 2009 study found, not surprisingly, that factors ranging from clothing style to posture play a role in how impressions are formed. Another 2011 study found that a limp handshake can make you appear overly passive. In the hiring process, interviewers may think they're making logical, grounded judgments, but their efficiency-seeking brain has built-in biases that influence judgment.

It may not feel fair, but it's how the brain works. Recall that your brain likes ease and conserving energy.

So, when you meet a new person, the brain looks for shortcuts. Since it takes time to get to know someone, your brain is looking at clues, then filling in the blanks with assumptions that it deems true. We don't just do this with people. Think about the last time you toured an open house. Many homeowners will go to great inconvenience and expense to have someone "stage" their home so it looks most appealing. Never mind that staged homes don't reflect how people truly live (no clutter, cookies baking in the oven, ridiculously clean closets). Our emotional brain makes us want to pay top dollar for a staged house, and pass—or offer a lower bid—on an honestly lived-in house. Similarly, if you're trading in or selling your car, you're likely to have it detailed, despite the fact that *shiny* doesn't correlate with *quality*.

We can't eliminate unconscious biases, but we can become more aware of them and create workarounds. For example, recent studies have shown that corporate diversity training doesn't create lasting changes. What does help are systems and processes that remove the opportunity to apply our deep biases. For example, some companies use technology to filter résumés to remove names, ages, and gender references, leaving only experience.

Your overprotective brain is a faultfinder: it scans the environment and looks for fault every one-fifth of a second. Instead of resenting the fact that people constantly make negative assumptions about us, we can work to improve how we're perceived. When it comes to observable traits, we can make some changes almost instantly: we can change how we dress, sit, stand, shake hands, and make eye contact. Other changes to our physiology take more time and effort: losing weight, sleeping better, and improving self-regulation so we respond mindfully and appropriately rather than impulsively.

When I began working with Jessica, she had a loud inner voice telling her she wasn't good enough, despite the fact that her boss and her boss's boss constantly gave her positive feedback and great reviews. She traced it back to her father's beliefs about her potential when she was growing up. She compared herself to others in the workplace and felt less polished, less confident, less outspoken, and more frumpy. She described her fashion choices as Garanimals (a line of color-coded children's clothes dating from the 1970s).

During our time together Jessica took on the following practices to change her outer state:

- She joined JumpstartMD and got personalized coaching and support to lose forty pounds in four months.
- She worked with a Nordstrom personal shopper to update her wardrobe.
- She got a flattering haircut, changing the style she'd worn for years.
- She continued her boxing practice, which gives her strength and a sense of power. Most people have no clue that she's strong enough to bench-press them, but she feels it and it carries into her emotional state. This practice also helps center her, and the strenuous exercise helps her reduce stress.

Your Outer Transformation Toolkit

1. **Work with a personal shopper.** I'm all about efficiency, so I do almost all my shopping online. However, I know from experience how much time a personal shopper can save. You send them your preferences and needs before the meeting. Then you enter a dressing room that already contains appropriate options, and you don't leave that room until you're done and have fabulous items. The consultant runs around the store for you. It's free at Nordstrom (and very low pressure).

2. **Get a great haircut.** This may involve breaking up with your current stylist. Not sure where to find a good one? Ask others for a referral. Just make sure you ask people who have great hair.

3. **Start a strength-training practice.** You'll get both health and emotional benefits. While personal trainers are great for those who like gyms and need an expert partner to push them, you can also do yoga at home, or work out with an inexpensive kettle ball or adjustable dumbbells.

4. **Get a makeover.** Learn how to apply makeup for day and evening. (Sorry gentlemen, unless you work in the makeup industry, this suggestion only applies to women. Perhaps one day, corporate America will embrace a less masculine look.) You can get high quality, free makeovers at any MAC or Sephora counter.

5. **Learn how you are seen.** Find trusted, confident people who aren't afraid to tell you the truth about how you're perceived by others.

Authentic Change

Some people would say that putting on different clothes or acting outside our typical pattern is inauthentic. The truth is, we're all constantly changing depending on what we pay attention to. The trick is to change intentionally, instead of accidentally reinforcing traits and behaviors that aren't aligned with our highest vision for ourselves. For example, without intention, most of us will become more distracted, overweight, impatient, and stressed. That's change for the worse. And when it comes to clothing, while you may love working from home in your pajamas, you clearly know better than to wear them to work.

Authenticity is about being real . . . not rigid. It's about being transparent about both your strengths and vulnerabilities. Authenticity is no license to act like a jerk, and it's not about stubbornly holding onto valued personality traits that aren't working. The most successful leaders figure out how to be gracefully and appropriately authentic. If you're unwilling to adapt to your audience, your career will hit a wall. It's a bit like saying: "I have this trait—I call it *putting a finger up my nose*—that helps me relax during stressful meetings. Some people tell me it's distracting and not good for my credibility, but it helps me focus so they should just get over it. Besides, I've always done it and I'm not about to change it just because others don't like it." In his blockbuster book *What Got You Here Won't Get You There*, Marshall Goldsmith calls this bad habit "An excessive need to be 'me': Exalting our faults as virtues simply because they're who we are."

Anyone Can Change

I once had the pleasure of working for an inspiring CIO who had to change the communication style that worked for him when he was a more junior leader. Three of his most dominant and prized traits were: passionate, quick-thinker, and extroverted communicator. Culled while growing up in the Middle East, and honed for business in New York City, these traits were part of a mixture that propelled him to success. It wasn't until he landed a job in Northern California, in a culture known for being "nice" and agreeable, that he ran into trouble. With the help of a coach, he quickly came to see that people were misunderstanding his intent. People interpreted his direct, passionate communication style as intimidating, closed-minded, and a sign of poor listening skills. His style masked qualities and values including flexibility and deep care for others. He could have claimed that these traits were "part of his DNA," and that to change would be inauthentic. But he cared more about being effective than being rigidly right. He started listening more and speaking less. And when he did speak, he learned to use a less declarative tone and language. He might preface comments with "I'm just tossing out a nascent thought and I want your suggestions."

Contrary to what you might have heard, your MBTI, DiSC, or SOCIAL STYLE is not etched in stone, and is certainly not an excuse for poor adaptability. You're responsible for your behaviors. Don't let them own you.

I once took on a client at the urging of my friend Angie. At the time, Angie was a vice president of technology at a global beverage company. She told me that her employee was close to getting fired because of his inability to work well with others, but she and the CIO wanted to make sure he had every chance to change. I don't typically take on projects like this one, but Angie was persistent, and she was aware that success was a long shot.

I used every tool I could think of. I brought out my tough love side, making it very clear what was at stake, and tried to help the client see how he was contributing to his own career demise. But I met my match in his stubbornness toward change. He was wedded to the idea that he was right and everyone else was wrong. Not only was his career about to careen off course, but his marriage was in shambles, and he hadn't spoken to his equally stubborn father in years. Rather than try to evolve his thoughts and beliefs in ways that would give him access to more collaborative behaviors, he blamed his behaviors on his heritage, claiming it was just his personality, and to change would be inauthentic.

I don't care who you are, where you came from, or what you've endured: anyone can change... but only if they want to.

WHEN CHANGE IS HARD

In this chapter, I've talked about outward traits that are relatively easy to change. Yet, nearly all my clients want to work on one body-related trait that is much more complex: sleep. This is so challenging that I'm devoting a whole chapter to it (see Chapter Six). If you've ever been passionate about achieving a personal health goal, then failed to do it, you already know just how hard it is to change. Part Two of this book will take you step-by-step through a process to help you overcome your brain's programming and achieve any desired behavioral change.

REFLECTION QUESTIONS

1. What do you know or suspect about how people perceive you upon first impression?

2. If you don't have solid evidence about others' first impressions of you, how can you learn?

3. What one thing do you want to change about how you present yourself to the world?

4. What traits and habits are you most proud of?
   - When do those traits serve you?
   - When do they get in the way?

CHAPTER FOUR:

Nurture Brilliant Relationships

Relationships are not simply the "icing on the cake"
for a life well lived. Relationships are the cake.

—Daniel J. Siegel, MD

A couple of weeks ago, I had a conversation with a senior vice president of a multibillion-dollar health-care company to debrief him on the group coaching program he recently sponsored. He was accustomed to investing hundreds of thousands of dollars in one-on-one coaching for his top leaders, but this was his first experience of group coaching. I was expecting him to ask questions about specific individuals: How engaged were they? What growth did I observe? Instead, he started with this question: "Can you tell me why people in this program are so damn appreciative of this experience? I've never seen anything like it from executives who get more expensive one-on-one coaching." I paused and said, "I love one-on-

one coaching, but something very special happens in a group. These people form trusting bonds within a couple of hours of the program. And they have conversations unlike anything they've experienced at work. They realize that, even though they work with these people (sometimes for years), they have never really known them."

Authentic relationships—where we feel safe to say anything, and feel seen, appreciated, and trusted—are like a crack hit to our brain (without the negative side effects). We get a flood of feel-good neurotransmitters including oxytocin and dopamine, and we strengthen our vagus nerve system, which, in turn, calms our sympathetic nervous system.

Gimme some of that any day.

Humor me for a minute and pause to think about a time in your past where you felt really engaged in your work; where time flew by and you looked forward to the day. If you don't have such a memory, think about a time in your personal life where you were most happy.

Got one?

Now, think about the people in your life at that time. What was the quality of your relationships? If you're anything like every workshop participant who's answered this question, it's likely that you had at least one trusting, easy relationship at work and home, where you felt like you could speak your mind without judgment; where laughter was abundant and conversations were easy. And it's also likely that you didn't have a toxic boss, spouse, colleague, or acquaintance.

We simply cannot be our most brilliant selves without supportive relationships—we're genetically wired to connect with others. Before we had the brain scans to prove this, Gallup proved it decades ago through their exhaustive research on employee engagement. They came up with twelve questions that measured how satisfied, motivated, and connected someone was at work. Among the questions was: "Do you have a best friend at work?" Sadly, in my experience, many executives found this question was trivial and left it out of employee engagement surveys. Now we have irrefutable science to prove its importance to our mental health and performance.

From an evolutionary standpoint, the most important aspect to survival is the ability to develop relationships with others. John Medina, author of *Brain Rules*, explains, "Our ability to understand each other is our chief survival tool. Relationships helped us survive in the jungle and are critical to surviving at work and school today." Despite the fact that our well-being depends upon fulfilling connections with others, startlingly, twenty-five percent of Americans cannot name a single person they feel close to (according to a 2006 Purdue University study). We are experiencing a loneliness epidemic.

In our era of social media, it's easy to stay informed and semi-connected. But social media platforms like Facebook and Instagram aren't a substitute for real connections. While we may get a nice little dopamine hit every time we click "like" or get liked back, these platforms actually cause us pain—the pain of comparison and inferiority. Some have dubbed the simultaneous feelings of congratulation and envy we often experience upon seeing a friend's shiny life as "frenvy." A study at Denmark's Happiness Research Institute found that people who gave up Facebook for one week reported suffering less envy and being "more satisfied" with their lives than those who continued using the site.

When we feel ostracized, lonely, or misunderstood, the same part of the brain lights up (the dorsal anterior cingulate cortex, or dACC) that would if we hammered our thumb. Neuroscientists refer to this relationship-based pain as "social pain." Social pain may be worse than physical pain, because while your sprained ankle will heal, your mind repeats the thoughts and feelings associated with social pain over and over, igniting the pain center of your brain each time. And social pain manifests as physical pain *in addition* to psychological and emotional pain. Anyone who's experienced "heartache," "heartbreak," or "homesickness" knows that those terms are more than metaphor: they aptly describe our experience of physical distress. More bad news about social pain: according to Amy Banks, author of *Wired to Connect: The Surprising Link Between Brain Science and Strong, Healthy Relationships,* relationships with people who don't understand you may weaken neural circuits that enable you to connect in healthier ways. In other words, being in unhealthy relationships negatively affects your brain, making it more difficult to create healthy relationships. Toxic encounters switch on our SNS (sympathetic nervous system), putting our brains into a threat state where we're less able to access our "intelligent" brain, the prefrontal cortex. Our adrenals pump cortisol (stress hormone) into our system, increasing our heart rate, anxiety, and overall stress. Long-term exposure to toxic relationships will lead to physical and emotional burnout.

To live a brilliant life, we must attract and nourish relationships that make us happier, healthier, and more effective in all areas of life. We need people who make us laugh; pick us up on a bad day and remind us of our brilliance; trust us with their deepest thoughts and feelings; listen without judgment or trying to fix us; own their faults and accept ours; are easy to be around; encourage us to strive for greatness through their words and own example; and help us reframe troubling thoughts so we can see new possibilities. We need connections with loving, trusting, dependable people who are willing to be vulnerable. And everyone needs at least one friend they can call at 3:00 AM in an emergency, knowing this person won't hesitate to come to their rescue.

This chapter will help you assess the quality of your relationships, and take steps to improve them, so you can be your most calm, centered, happy, healthy, productive—brilliant—self.

The Pain of Invisibility

When asked what superpower they'd most like to have, most people name flight or invisibility. Yet feeling "invisible" in the eyes of others is one of the most painful experiences one can have.

In my senior year of high school, five of my best friends viciously turned on me. They spread rumors about me, threw wadded up nastygram notes at me, and excluded me. But the most painful thing they did was ignore me, acting as though I didn't exist, even though we were mere inches apart. They did the same to another girl, Kristy. While part of me felt bad for Kristy, another was so grateful to have an ally. Kristy (who went on to work for the United Nations helping rebuild countries devastated by war and natural disaster) devised a way for us to bond and make light of the situation: we'd touch a finger to the tip of our nose—our secret signal that we had cloaked ourselves in invisibility. Kristy's friendship was a salve that helped me get through a dark time. Too many people go through bullying alone, and a tragic number take their own lives.

TAKE TIME TO TRULY "SEE" OTHERS

Feeling unseen can leave us feeling as though we don't exist. In her book, *Fierce Conversations*, Susan Scott describes a tribal greeting, where, upon encountering another person, the members say *sawubona*, which means, "I see you." The response is *sikhona*, "I am seen." It's as if to say, until you see me, I am not here. Sure beats "Hi, how ya doin'?" said as we pass by quickly, looking at our phones. (I think the award-winning movie *Avatar* may have had an anthropologist on the team because the highly connected and spiritual inhabitants of planet Pandora greet each other with, "I see you." Meanwhile, the invading humans leave a trail of pain, greed, and destruction.) There's something so deeply mystical about this greeting. This tribe's wisdom preceded quantum theory, which holds that outcomes do not exist until observed or measured. (For mind-bending quantum fun, check out the thought experiment called "Schrödinger's cat.")

When I see homeless people, I feel deep sadness for their isolation. Just yesterday, I drove past a man with a sign reading, "Seeking human kindness." While I don't always give money, I do try to smile and make eye contact. I want them to know I see them. And I strive to imagine them as strong, worthy people in a rough patch they need to go through to get to the next phase of life, rather than pitiful. I hope this energy comes through. So, how do you see others? How do you see those closest to you? Reverence or resentment? Curiosity or assumed knowing? Compassion or annoyance?

One doesn't have to be alone or ignored to feel soul-crushing loneliness. Many people feel lonely in their marriages. Being misunderstood or judged by those closest to us is the worst kind of social pain. We often misunderstand those we've known for a long time because we lose our curiosity. We say painful things like "I knew you were going to do/say that," or, "You always do that." Because your brain likes shortcuts, and because no two brains filter information the same way, misunderstandings happen all the time. It takes practice, empathy, curiosity, and deep listening to come even close to truly understanding someone—something your efficiency-seeking brain would rather not do, even though it's critical to the health of your connections with others. If people truly did take the time to listen and understand, we'd have less need for people to pay coaches and therapists to listen.

> *If you understood everything I said, you'd be me.*
> —MILES DAVIS

The healthiest relationships maintain a sense of curiosity about their partner: seeing them as a beautiful, evolving mystery, worthy of interest and deep listening. Two dear friends of mine have been together nearly twenty years, but when I'm with them, you'd think they are newly together in the way they partner, speak to each other, and listen. The wife is an expert in a personality assessment called the Enneagram. While she and I were talking about the instrument and our types, she said, "I still don't know what type my husband is." She could easily have labeled him, but she chose curiosity instead.

How to Recognize and Sustain Brilliant Relationships

When it comes to evaluating whether someone is a good person for you to enfold/keep in your tribe, consider three questions:

HOW DO YOU FEEL AROUND THIS PERSON?

You don't have to be friends with everyone in the office, or all of the parents of your kids' friends. When it comes to relationships, quality is definitely better than quantity. As you meet new people, note how you feel after the interaction. Is there mutual trust and respect? What was the feeling you left with? Was there laughter? Was it the kind of laughter that isn't at the expense of someone else, but that lightens the mood in a non-harmful way? Is the tone one of complaining? If so, are they going through a tough time and in need of a sounding board, or is this their habitual mood? Are they more focused on problems or possibility? Blame or accountability? Anger and judgment, or compassion and acceptance?

To live brilliantly and experience deep trust, love, joy, and empathy, we need to have connections with people who have vibrational energies as high or higher than ourselves. If that sounds too "woo-woo" for you, let me put it another way. Think of someone close to you. How do you feel when you are with that person? Calm, happy,

Great minds discuss ideas; *average minds discuss* events; *small minds discuss* people.

—ELEANOR ROOSEVELT

understood, and valued . . . or anxious, resentful, and misunderstood? Ease or stress? Now try this. Divide your closest peers and family members into two groups:

1. Those who lift you up and make you a better person—who see and accept you for who you are—and

2. those who bring you down, who leave you with a sense of unease and often a feeling of being misunderstood.

When was the last time you told people in the first group how much you appreciate them?

Now let's address the second group. Being around toxic energy is stressful. We can feel constriction in our chest, anxiety about what's going to happen next, and a sense of being trapped. Yet, many of us hold on to toxic relationships out of fear, guilt, or a sense of obligation. Sean Stephenson, author of the awesome book *Get Off Your "But,"* describes three forms of toxic people: drainers, takers, and destroyers. Drainers exhaust us with their seemingly constant drama of emotions including anger, rage, or jealousy. Or they tire us with constant complaining or gossiping. Takers instead drain our resources, including time and money. There's always an imbalance, with them always on the receiving side. Destroyers don't want us to better ourselves. They will mock our healthy habits or our efforts to learn, grow, and achieve. Destroyers want us to party with them all the time, quit school, or miss deadlines. They'll mock us for reading instead of watching TV. There's nothing wrong with fun and silliness (I specialize in both) but for destroyers, it's not about having fun; it's about keeping you low, so they don't feel the pain of comparison when you better yourself.

If you want to thrive, you must cut toxic people from your life. If that sounds harsh, it's nothing compared to what they're doing to your mental state and your potential to better yourself. There's no one right way or time to do this. Sometimes you can just quietly lose contact. Other times, you need to say something. If the latter, be brief, clear, and compassionate. Use "I" language versus more blaming "you" language, as in: "I don't feel good in this relationship and I need to distance myself," versus "You constantly bring me down."

If you're in a toxic marriage, I'm all for trying to learn communication skills, improve yourself, and work to improve the situation. But if you've tried everything and nothing changes, your life depends on you getting out eventually. Please know that I understand just how difficult that is. My ex-husband and I stayed together years beyond the unofficial end of our marriage. Now, as co-parents and friends, we've finally found emotional ease and freedom in the right relationship.

WHO DOES THIS PERSON HELP YOU BECOME?

Our relationships drive us to become better, or keep us stuck and stagnant. Social research shows that we adopt the habits of those around us. If your group of closest friends overeats and smokes, they're not likely to support your goal to cut back and get healthy because it will feel threatening to them. If your closest friends gossip, it's difficult to abstain from the toxic banter. It's rare that we wake up one day and decide to get our nose pierced and an arm sleeve tattoo unless our closest friends and family have done so and normalized this.

The question is not whether our habits and behaviors are good or bad (you can have as many tattoos and piercings as you want and be incredibly inspirational and successful), but rather:

- How are your habits helping you be your best self?
- How are your habits holding you back from fulfilling your potential?
- What do you know you need to (reluctantly) change? Who can support you in this change?
- Whom must you surround yourself with so you can be your best self?

You don't have to break up with people who aren't helping you be your best self, but you do need to become conscious of how you spend your time. And you may need to develop new connections through networking groups in your field of interest.

WHAT'S THE LEVEL OF MUTUAL SUPPORT?

Look back at your list of closest connections and ask, "Could I call this person in the middle of the night in an emergency?" Then ask, "Would this person be likely to call me in the middle of the night in an emergency?" Meaningful relationships are mutually supportive. If you or someone else is constantly asking for help but not readily delivering it, your relationship is lopsided. And if your answer to the question is anything but yes for at least one person in your network, you don't have the relationship you need to truly thrive.

Tips for Connecting with New People

I marvel at extroverts who can walk into any room and strike up a conversation. For the rest of us, cocktail parties or other gatherings can cause anxiety. "What will we talk about?" "What if people don't like me?" "What if I forget everyone's names?" I'm naturally terrible at small talk. I prefer "big talk" where we share hopes, fears, pitfalls, and triumphs. But there's a happy medium, where we can connect lightly and authentically until trust creates a bridge where truly meaningful conversations can happen.

BE CURIOUS AND OTHER-FOCUSED

My favorite question to ask when I meet someone for the first time is, "Where are you from?" It's particularly vague—as opposed to "Where were you born?"—so the person can answer in myriad ways that will give you a glimpse into how they view their past. Here's another great one: "Tell me your story." You'll likely get a big pause after you ask this. Don't fill the space by speaking.

Let them gather their thoughts. This question (actually a statement but the brain hears it like a question) is a rare gift that permits them to reflect on their path and share important milestones with a curious person. I love to see where people start this one. Do they begin with work? With an early memory? What's the tone of the narrative: gratitude, remorse, resentment, anger, or love?

LISTEN AND FIND SIMILARITIES

We're wired to detect differences. Still, the brain doesn't need much to create that much-desired tribal connection. When I walk into a client's office, I see evidence of what's meaningful to them. They might have family photos, awards, sayings, and books. I get genuinely curious and ask questions. People have these things on display because they reflect what brings them meaning. When I ask them about the people in the pictures or the books on the shelf, I am honoring what matters to them. And I can always find something that we have in common. Even a messy desk is an opportunity for me to express commonality.

BE VULNERABLE

No one is perfect. Be willing to laugh at yourself and admit fault. Since our brains are constantly comparing ourselves to others, this makes you safer to talk with. It's also a sign that you trust this person, which in turn, will make them feel valued and more inclined to trust you back.

MAKE EYE CONTACT

Here's a simple practice you can start today: the next time you walk down the street, smile and make eye contact with people. I sometimes add a practice from Deepak Chopra's *The Spontaneous Fulfillment of Desire*: during the day, as I encounter strangers, I will silently say to myself, "Namaste," a beautiful Sanskrit term, roughly translated as "The divine in me recognizes the divine in you."

I used to be painfully shy around strangers. Then, when I was in a coaching program, I decided to change. I made a practice of smiling at and making eye contact with strangers until I altered my brain. I recall one day, walking down the street in San Francisco, I saw a man and woman who appeared confused as they looked down at a map. People walked by them as if they weren't there. I knew then that I had changed my brain because I felt this desire to help them. I moved forward with confidence and compassion and said, "Can I help you find something?" Turns out they were French, so I used my very rusty skills to speak to them in their language. (Hopefully I sent them in the right direction!) We all benefitted from this serendipitous exchange, and I helped them feel like the city was a bit more approachable. With repetition, I rewired my brain. Now I make a point of making eye contact with people I would have ignored in the past: homeless people, vendors trying to share their work, and volunteers hoping I will stop and help their cause. And I'm a compliment dispenser; I can't help myself from commenting on positive traits I see in strangers as we stand in line. I'm not sure who benefits more—them or me.

Attracting Brilliant Relationships

To attract the relationships I've described in this chapter, we must become the kind of person we desire in our lives. What are you bringing to relationships? Be honest with yourself. If you're constantly in quarrels with others, the common denominator is you. If you feel like others don't trust you with their full selves, look at how trusting and vulnerable you are with others. If others complain or gossip to you, assess how often you do the same. Then instead of confronting others about their behaviors, fix your own. Your relationships are a reflection of you. If you aren't happy with the quality of your relationships, what qualities will you improve in yourself?

> *There is only one corner of the universe you can be certain of improving, and that's your own self.*
>
> —Aldous Huxley

Your Brilliant Relationship Assessment

Below is a checklist to assess how well you're managing your thoughts and actions to build and sustain brilliant relationships.

- How often and openly do I tell people how much I care and appreciate them?
- How forgiving am I? Grudges fill us with toxicity and drive a wedge between others and ourselves.
- How well do I listen to others without judgment or trying to fix them?

- How generous am I with my time, attention, knowledge, and network?
- How often do I give (genuine) compliments to friends and strangers?
- How often do I give the benefit of the doubt? (That person with the scowl? Perhaps she has a headache. The boastful bore? Perhaps he's overcompensating for insecurity.) When we shift our story to one of acceptance and compassion, we shift our tone to one that's more likely to create trust. You'd want others to do the same for you on your worst days.
- How well do I seek out new friends in places that I like to frequent (workshops, yoga classes, dance floors, wine tastings, etc.)?

If you don't like your answers, take steps to improve your relationships today.

REFLECTION QUESTIONS

1. What positive qualities do you bring to your relationships?

2. What qualities do you want to practice more?

3. What negative qualities do you bring to your relationships?

4. What qualities do you want to practice less?

5. Which of your close relationships is toxic?

6. When will you cut them from your life with grace, freeing both of you?

7. Thinking about your closest friends, who among them help you to be a better, happier person?

8. If you don't have such friends, what steps will you take to find them?

CHAPTER FIVE:

Manage Your Relationship with "Stuff"

How we spend our days is, of course,
how we spend our lives.

—ANNIE DILLARD

Victor had me laughing within five minutes of our first conversation. His boss had hired me as a coach with hopes that I could help him work at a more strategic level, delegating more of the day-to-day operations to his team. Victor loves helping people, and being a nice, helpful, affable guy is core to his identity. People took advantage of his open-door policy, stopping by often to ask him questions. Thanks to his extroverted personality, those conversations tended to go on for a long time. Victor actually relished the interruptions because he loved helping, he loved conversing, and less obviously, it gave him an excuse to avoid work that was important but outside his sweet spot. If Victor was to ever rise to the level his boss and other executives wanted, he'd have to make some difficult shifts in how he used his time, and he'd have to make significant progress on neglected strategic projects.

This last of the Brilliance realms includes our relationship to our spaces, possessions, technology, and time. We maximize the potential in this realm when we eliminate clutter and increase beauty and functionality around us, use technology wisely and mindfully to fulfill our goals and connect with others, and organize our days so we achieve our highest goals.

Managing Your Time

When you went to bed last night, how'd you feel about your day? Were you pleased about what you accomplished? Or did you feel like much was left unaddressed or unfinished? How confident are you that at the end of today you can look back and say that it was productive and fulfilling? When we operate optimally in this realm, we move through our day with calm, purposeful efficiency, like a captain steering a boat, confident in his destination, gracefully avoiding obstacles beneath the surface.

Most of us don't plan our days mindfully. To your brain, almost nothing is more energy-consuming than planning a well-lived day. How on earth are you to prioritize when so many things are important, not to mention out of your control?

Because prioritization is painful, we often don't actually *choose* how to spend our time: we let life *happen to us.* We do the easy thing, like rolling out of bed and checking e-mail while the coffee is brewing. Productivity is about making deliberate choices over and over again throughout your day. It's about strategically saying yes and no to activities based on your values, needs, goals, and limitations.

In case you aren't already familiar with your limitations, here are the big two:

1. **Time:** We have twenty-four hours in a day and an unknown, finite amount of days to live. No matter how much you add to your to-do list, you get no additional seconds in the day. And taking time away from sleep does you little good because the second limitation is . . .

2. **Physical:** We have bodies (and brains) that need constant nourishment, water, sleep, and repair. When these elements aren't sufficient, our bodies suffer and can eventually break down in catastrophic ways. Many of us have injuries or illnesses that further limit us. We all have brains that, while amazingly powerful and complex, are in many ways quite delicate and limited.

Years ago, at a talk by author and neuroleadership expert David Rock, I learned that some neuroscientists believe that on average, we have about ninety minutes of good prefrontal cortex time. That means that for about an hour a day—maybe two—we think clearly and efficiently. The rest of the day is a haul, where we struggle to focus and retain and recall information. Lack of sleep, water, caffeine, and nourishment shrink that small productivity window even further. If we aren't honest about our limitations, we cannot be productive. While ninety minutes may not sound like a lot, think about your past week for a moment and imagine if, at the end of every day, you were able to look back and say that, for about two (consecutive or non-consecutive) hours each day, you were able to do high-quality work against a project that is vitally important to your highest goals, values, and potential. For me, I know that if I did two hours of quality writing, in addition to caring for my health, daughter, dog, and supporting my clients, I would be deeply satisfied.

When we understand and acknowledge our limitations, and then strategically craft our day to work with them—not against them—we can step toward our potential. The following are "hacks" you can make to your schedule, body, and environment so you can be your most productive, focused self every day.

UPGRADE YOUR "TO-DO" LIST

Most of our to-do lists are created haphazardly, without considering our vital values, priorities, and goals. In order to get where you want to go (in your day and, eventually, in your life), you need a well-designed map. At the beginning of each day, do the following:

1. **List your biggest projects:** Write between one to three major works in progress that are most vital to your success. Under or beside each project heading, list actions that must happen today to move them forward.

2. **Identify people you need to communicate with:** Write the names of people you either need to hear from or deliver to.

3. **Record vital tasks:** Write down any other tasks that *must* happen today before you go to sleep. Block (realistic) time on your calendar for these tasks.

4. **Purposefully scan e-mail:** When you open your e-mail, look for those names you wrote down first and read and write e-mails only to those people. Then scan for any e-mails marked urgent. *Then close e-mail.*

5. **Make your top priorities non-negotiable:** Live your day as though your life depends on getting your top actions accomplished. In this and later chapters you'll learn how to manage distractions, align your tasks to your values, and graciously decline requests.

PAUSE AND CHOOSE YOUR NEXT TASK

Much of the time, we flow from task to task almost unconsciously, operating out of habit and ease: we watch the next episode of whatever Netflix show has sucked us in, realizing too late that we traded entertainment for sleep; we get caught up in e-mail for an hour, when we only meant to send one message; we curate photo albums for Facebook when something else more vital was calling for our attention; we accept back-to-back meetings even when our presence isn't required. If we want to have productive, fulfilling days, we must mindfully choose how we spend our time. In addition to planning your day, try pausing at the completion of one task, then consciously choose where to best focus your limited attention. In his book *Two Awesome Hours*, author Josh Davis calls this pause a "decision point." When we pause and choose our next task deliberately, we're more likely to get important work done, and less likely to be pulled into the vortex of e-mail or social media or other distractions. It may also keep us from doing work that's satisfying, but better done at another time or by someone else. Or it may save us from doing work that's easy but not important.

This may sound like a simple or easy thing to do. I've found that it's neither. After trying this for weeks, I now find that I am in the habit of stopping after finishing a task, and saying (sometimes out loud), "What to do next?" Before, I would have just plowed on to the next shiny, easy thing and savored the feeling of checking it off my to-do list. Planning your day in advance will help guide your choices, but it will take repetition for this pause to become habitual, so you don't look back on your day and wonder why you didn't get to your most vital tasks.

WORK ON YOUR MOST IMPORTANT TASK EARLY IN THE DAY

Activities deplete and reinvigorate us differently, and reading e-mail is one of the most brain-depleting activities. Every e-mail has the potential to add to our to-do list, surprise us, and cause an emotional threat response. So when you check e-mail early in the day (one client recently admitted he checks e-mail before he even gets out of bed), you're depleting your brainpower before you even tackle a tough project. If we want to have brilliantly productive days, we must do the hard thing early. We can thank Mark

Twain for this disturbing but memorable metaphor for avoiding procrastination:

> *Eat a live frog first thing in the morning*
> *and nothing worse will happen to you*
> *the rest of the day.*

It feels so damn good to check tasks off to-do lists, that most of us busy ourselves on the wrong things. When we avoid the hard but important thing, we fill ourselves with stress, guilt, the sense of being overwhelmed, and eventually, regret. Schedule your day so you have space to focus on the hard thing first. You'll feel more in control, calm, proud, and able to take on the remaining tasks without the residue of guilt. When writing this book, I experimented (and procrastinated) for months before I figured out how to get a sixty-to-ninety-minute chunk of focused writing time. I learned that I needed to set the alarm (and coffeepot) for 4:45 AM. This gave me time to write before I spent up to twenty minutes reading and sending priority e-mails, then shifting into "mom mode." It was painful at first (I normally rise at around 6:30 AM), but the sense of accomplishment each day made it worth it. I also had to adjust my bedtime so I went to sleep shortly after my daughter did.

Managing Time Toolkit

DAILY TIME INVENTORY

Most of us have phones and other devices that track our sleep and steps. But what if we tracked how we spent our time over the course of one day? In the resources section of my web site (www.BrillianceInc.com/Resources), you'll find my own time tracking tool. It instructs you to measure activities by

- Duration

- Time of day

- How tactical or strategic they are

- Your emotional state while doing the task

- Whether it's something you could delegate

- Degree of ease versus difficulty

4-D Conversation

Conduct what I call a 4-D conversation with yourself, your team, or your family to prioritize and free up time.

1. **Drop**: What can you stop doing because it's not vital to you living brilliantly? Or, it's not vital to your team's success? Note, if you tell yourself you "should" do something, move it into one of two categories: drop or do.

2. **Delegate**: What must be done, but doesn't have to be done by you? Get creative. Nearly any task can be delegated. And doing so is often a gift to someone who is trying to grow, or whose livelihood as an independent business owner/freelancer depends on people like you.

3. **Do**: What *must* you do because any of the following are true: Only you can do it and it has to get done; you won't achieve your goals without doing it; or you have no choice but to do it?

4. **Do Differently**: What must be done, but can be done more efficiently? For example, why are meetings nearly always scheduled for an hour? What if you created an agenda then set the meeting duration accordingly?

Managing Your Physical Energy

I often hear people say, "I don't need breakfast" or "I don't have time to eat lunch," and I wonder, "Have they run that past their brain?" Because I can tell you that while *you* may have developed the habit of not eating, *your brain* isn't happy about it. Unless you're some kind of automaton, you need to fuel your brain with glucose. A disturbing study of judges' rulings discovered that they gave out more lenient sentences after eating a sandwich. On the flip side, judges delivered harsher sentences when hungry. And not surprisingly, the judges had no clue that biological needs played a role in decision-making: they thought they were being objective.

If you want to have energy through the morning, eat a high-protein, low-sugar breakfast. If you don't have much time, consider stealing my lazy, highly nutritious one-minute smoothie recipe that uses four ingredients (all of which can be delivered to your front door): Shakeology powder, a huge scoop of Vitamineral Green superfood powder, and cinnamon (all added to water, with ice for texture). Or, try a hard-boiled egg with avocado and black beans. While it may not be as delicious as that donut or muffin from Starbucks, you'll come to love the taste of whatever breakfast provides the fuel you need to be your most brilliant self. I advise all my clients to keep nuts handy at work, so they can have a brain-friendly, low-glycemic snack when hunger hits.

I'm guessing that many of your office colleagues are tired, hungry, stressed, and distracted. If you want to have productive meetings, consider bringing dark chocolate to share. The caffeine and sugar pack a powerful, positive punch. I love to hand out DOVE chocolates that come in pretty individually wrapped foil with a wise or whimsical thought inside the wrapper. If you have midday meetings, encourage people to bring lunch if they don't have time to eat before. Most of us let our calendar system dictate how long our meetings run by default. To reduce stress and honor people's physical and time limitations, schedule your meetings for less than an hour or half-hour, so people have time to take a restroom break between meetings.

MOVE STRATEGICALLY

You don't have to go to a gym. You don't even have to break a sweat. But you do need to move. Your brain works more efficiently shortly after exertion. Even just fifteen minutes of modest exertion—like climbing stairs, or walking around your building—will help. Exercise was one more thing that Victor, who you met earlier, was neglecting. Because he valued human connection so much, he decided to conduct as many meetings as possible walking around lovely Lake Merritt—about a fifty-minute walk.

Managing Your Environment

Open space planning—where people sit close to one another without walls—is one of the more unfortunate trends in business because it's so detrimental to productivity and focus. As author and Neuroleadership founder David Rock once said, "Primates hate crowding." I'd add, "Primates need quiet."

My client Lisa was struggling with maintaining focus without interruptions. Her desk was in a high-traffic area, and her employees often stopped by for advice. Lisa didn't want to be rude, but she was finding that her only productive time happened when she worked from home. She needed to signal to people that certain times were "open door" times, and others were "closed door" focus periods. Lisa explained to people her intention to carve out ninety minutes a day to work on projects, and the rest, she'd be available for consult. By doing this, she also set a positive example for others, giving them permission to do the same. She scheduled her focus time early in the day and held meetings in the afternoon when social needs are higher and prefrontal cortexes tired. Just so people would be certain about whether she was "in" or "out" she put up a small humorous sign reading: "Extrovert practicing introverted behaviors." Victor, who works in an office, put this sign on his door: "People-person performing torturous planning work." For more about working your schedule around your natural rhythm, check out Tony Schwartz's *The Way We're Working Isn't Working*.

Lisa also got sound-reducing headphones and a small lamp to brighten her workspace. When possible, she reserved conference space so she could spread her work out and focus in private. She also created Pandora stations with music that helped her focus. Music that works for one person may distract another. I like to work to instrumental music (although I start my day with sacred choral music). Experiment to find what works best for you. A small study in 2014 found that when people listened to music they liked, the default mode section of the brain lit up. This part of the brain helps us switch our focus to our internal thoughts, making it easier to focus. So go ahead and try working to whatever pleases you . . . including silence.

WORKING AT HOME

Many of us work at home periodically. If you want to be brilliantly productive at home, you need an environment that's organized, beautiful, peaceful, and supportive. Most of us have closets, attics, and drawers overflowing with stuff we no longer need. If you want to feel a great sense of relief, bag up all items you haven't used in six months and call a charity to pick them up from your curb. This will help tremendously, but you're still likely to have piles of mail and work. Remove clutter from spaces where you need to think, even if you have to shove it unceremoniously into a drawer, closet, or cabinet. I use storage ottomans in my office for items I don't need to reference often. Clearing clutter (even as simple as cleaning out a junk drawer) leaves you feeling more in control, like you can make things happen. For example, when we make our beds in the morning, it helps us start the day with a sense of control, completion, and order. Even if you don't work from home, you'll benefit from reduced stress if you come home to a peaceful environment that isn't begging to be tidied up.

I work from home a great deal of the time, and I'm very sensitive to my environment. When I first moved into my home, I didn't feel a sense of comfort and ease. I hired a painter to cover nearly every surface of my house (walls, ceilings, hearths—even the inside of my fireplaces) in colors that were pleasing and soothing. I arranged furniture according to feng shui principles (you can hire an expert for little cost) so energy flowed well and I felt a sense of ease. I don't have any fake plants in my home. Instead, I have orchids in almost every room. They last months and need very little water and light.

MATCH YOUR ENVIRONMENT TO THE TASK

Too often, we sit at a desk and get stuck or frustrated because we aren't efficient. If you want to be productive and experience that sense of flow, where time passes quickly and productively, you need to adjust your setting to the work.

When you need to innovate, problem-solve, and think strategically, don't try to do it at your desk. For one, that time you block off on your calendar is likely to get usurped by meetings and interruptions. Moreover, we can't plan innovation; we can only create the space for it. Frame your situation with a problem statement, then let go. Go on a hike, take a shower, or listen to music on your commute. Take a recording device with you so you can capture ideas. When I got stuck recently, realizing I needed to completely change direction on a project that was due in a week, I didn't sit down and edit immediately. Instead, I reviewed the new information, then let it stew for a couple of days, jotting down ideas as they came. If I was on a hike with my dog, I recorded the ideas in my phone. If I was driving, I jotted them down in a notebook once parked. Eventually, the puzzle pieces came together and I envisioned the new design.

When you need to focus on a task, create an interruption-free zone—turn off your e-mail, phone, IM program, and any screen that is superfluous to your primary task. It may help to tell others what you are doing so you don't worry about responding immediately. Research led by Gloria Mark (Professor in the Department of Informatics at the University of California, Irvine) showed that after an interruption, it takes an average of twenty-three minutes and fifteen seconds to refocus. That's assuming you don't get interrupted during that time. Note what time of day you do your best thinking and protect that time, saving it for your most important work. So, set a timer and work diligently until it goes off (keeping drinks and healthy snacks handy).

Managing Technology (so it doesn't manage you)

My clients are bombarded with hundreds of e-mails daily, and if that's not bad enough, they're expected to have instant messaging on all day as well. Finding time to focus or think is becoming harder and harder. Research has

> *The brain is a sequential processor, unable to pay attention to two things at the same time. Businesses and schools praise multitasking, but research clearly shows that it reduces productivity and increases mistakes.*
>
> —JOHN MEDINA, Brain Rules

shown that just having a phone on and nearby causes our attention to split, resulting in a ten percent IQ drop.

Most of us don't use technology as much as we let it use us. It's like we've put the technology in control and we're running on autopilot. We do this for three primary reasons: first, because we can. If, like me, you were born in or before the 1970s, you didn't grow up with the option to binge-watch TV, swipe screens on your smartphone, or watch videos anywhere, anytime. We had to actually work at entertaining ourselves. It takes incredible willpower to resist this technology overwhelm. And since human willpower is puny, we have to actually put rituals, rules, and structures in place if we are to stand a chance at resisting the draw of our devices.

A second reason we don't manage technology: it's easy and pleasurable, thus addictive. Your brain likes pleasure. Your brain likes ease. So, your brain says, "Go ahead and watch that next episode of our favorite show. You deserve it." Your brain doesn't mind that it means less sleep, learning, creating, connection, or movement. The more you repeat the behavior, the deeper the habit is embedded—the more episodes you binge-watch.

And a third reason we're addicted to our technology and mobile devices? We have too much to do. Tim was a new client who'd just been promoted into a huge job. He was performing so well, senior leadership gave him another interim job that they trusted only him to manage. Tim was always very focused and attentive on our calls, but when I talked with his peers, I learned that in large group meetings, he was head-down in his devices, tapping out e-mails, and failing to speak up in meetings. This was taking a huge toll on his credibility and connections with his peers. They saw him as aloof, and they assumed he felt more important than them. After all, they had lots of work to do as well, but they managed to get it done without multitasking in meetings. Tim was working on very high visibility projects, and had no one on his team that the top leadership trusted enough to sit in for him. He'd have to learn to prioritize his work better, delegate as much as he could, and recruit a very strong copilot, capable of sitting in for him on important meetings, so he could be fully in one place at a time.

Ideas for Taming Technology

- When you need to focus on work, close your door and exit all unnecessary apps and windows. Turn e-mail and notifications back on during designated times, or after vital work is completed.
- Turn off sound notifications (especially those telling you about a new e-mail or Facebook post).
- Tell people when you're planning to go "off the grid" so they know how long they'll need to wait for a response, and are less likely to come knocking or get impatient.
- Sleep without a phone nearby. If you do have a phone for music or a clock, set it to "do not disturb." You can adjust privacy settings so it will ring if certain people call. If you use your phone as a clock, replace it with an actual clock at night, and a watch during the day.
- Leave your phone behind when you attend meetings. You'll feel and appear more interested and engaged.
- If you're the leader, create "no phone zone" meetings. If people do bring them, ask that they turn them off.

- When you're having a conversation with another person, turn to face them (if it's a face-to-face conversation), and regardless of whether it's a live or virtual talk, shut off your computer screen and set your phone to "do not disturb."

Turning off your devices won't be easy at first. You'll feel compelled to check them continually. Notice this feeling and how it's evidence of addiction. One client of mine—a self-proclaimed workaholic—used to work and do e-mail until very late at night, sometimes until 2:00 AM. Her goals during our coaching program included working smarter, being seen more as a leader than a doer, and exercising more. Her brilliant experiment? First, she declined any meetings where her presence wasn't critical. (We'll cover more about how to say no with grace, not guilt, in Chapter Ten.) This freed up more than two hours a day where she could focus on important work she would have done at home in the evening. She also left her laptop at work and walked the two miles back to her house, carrying a small satchel with essential belongings, including a phone in case she was urgently needed.

Reduce Your Exposure to Toxic Energy

For better or worse, I'm incredibly sensitive to my environment. I pick up on negative energies easily and they cling to me, causing me anxiety. After I had my daughter, I became even more sensitive to energy, events, sights, smells, and sounds. I could no longer watch intense

TV shows containing violence and conflict, including so-called news. Nor can I work among great amounts of clutter (though I'm okay if it's out of sight, as you'd see if you opened my desk drawers).

I think we're all greatly affected by these things, yet some of us have become desensitized and don't realize the effect it has on us. My young daughter once unintentionally watched the news at her great-grandparents' home. Afterward, she looked at me with eyes wide with fear and said, "Mom, everything was horrible." Adults are often desensitized to the horrors and tactics of the news industry. The news is not designed to inform you; it's designed to instill fear, anger, and uncertainty, so you stay tuned and keep coming back. Without controversy, their ad sales would plummet. So they invent—and foment—controversy. You don't need this toxicity. I haven't watched news shows in more than fifteen years, yet news is inescapable unless you sequester yourself off the grid. To learn more about what media, books, and music provide toxic energy and positive energy, check out the book *Power vs. Force* by David Hawkins, heavily referenced in the more well-known *The Power of Intention* by Dr. Wayne Dyer. I get my news by reading, which puts me more in control of what I consume. My favorite source of information is *The Week* magazine.

Here are two actions you can take to help improve your emotional state, starting today:

1. **Take a TV news fast.** And choose sources that lean more toward informing, and less toward grabbing and keeping your attention.

2. **Take a social media fast.** Instead, read something inspiring and informative on blogs like PicktheBrain.com, brainpickings.com, lifehack.

com, and LinkedIn Pulse. Or listen to a great podcast while you take a walk—that's the best kind of multitasking. My favorite podcast at the moment is "The Tim Ferriss Show." It contains loads of informative, inspiring interviews with the most successful, productive, and interesting people in the world about their beliefs, habits, routines, and failures that helped them get to where they are now. Or, just pick up the phone and have a live, stress-reducing connection with another human being. When you do log on to Facebook, use it for what it's best designed to do: connect with humans in a way that has us feeling closer and more content. Set a timer for ten minutes (max) then move on to some other vital task.

You can be talented and brilliant intellectually, but if you're distracted, tired, and inefficient, you won't be as effective and respected as you can be. If you want to thrive at work and be seen as someone with executive presence who leads with power, grace, and inspiration, these are vital skills to acquire. Not only will you separate yourself from the masses who are frenetically working on the wrong things at the wrong time in subpar ways, you'll thrive mentally and emotionally.

REFLECTION QUESTIONS

1. Where are you working against your biological limits?

2. What one small thing will you do differently starting today to be more productive?

DAILY TIME/TASK INVENTORY

Write an inventory of how you spend your time in one day.

TIME	TASK	DURATION	(1) TACTICAL (10) STRATEGIC	SOMEONE ELSE COULD DO?	(1) EASY (10) HARD	FEELING STATE (1–10)

Larger version available at www.BrillianceInc.com/Resources

4-D TASK ASSIGNMENT

On a separate page, make a list of your daily, weekly, and monthly tasks. Then put them into one of the columns below.

There is nothing so useless as doing efficiently that which should not be done at all.

—PETER DRUCKER

DROP	DELEGATE	(MUST) DO	(DO) DIFFERENTLY
Things that are no longer worth doing given my own and the team's capacity, and the benefit of the task	Consider others' strengths, interests, and development goals	Things you will start or continue to do	How can you make tasks more efficient and effective?

Larger version available at www.BrillianceInc.com/Resources

4-D TASK ASSIGNMENT (PART TWO)

- Whose approval do you need?
- Who do you need to consult?
- Who do you need to inform?
- What support and resources do you need?

DAILY PLANNING TOOL

List your most important projects (no more than three)

1. _____

2. _____

3. _____

Who do you need to hear from?

Who do you need to contact? (When you open your e-mail, scan and send messages to the people listed above, then get to work on your most vital project before you read e-mail.)

What vital tasks *must* get completed before you go to sleep today?

CHAPTER SIX:

Brilliant Sleep

If healthy thirty-year-olds are sleep-deprived for six days (averaging, in the study, about four hours of sleep per night), parts of their body chemistry soon revert to that of a sixty-year-old. And if they are allowed to recover, it will take them almost a week to get back to their thirty-year-old system.

—JOHN MEDINA, *Brain Rules*

Sarah was one of my favorite bosses. She trusted me and gave me ample space to work independently. She was extremely supportive, singing my praises to leadership, and rewarding me whenever she could. We also became great friends, sharing many stories and laughter. But Sarah kept one thing hidden from me for years: she had horrible insomnia. While Sarah had many wonderful qualities, she also drove me crazy: her meetings were erratic, rarely had concrete agendas and outcomes, and even when they did, we seldom met the outcomes. And meetings always began late and ran long. It wasn't until later years that I learned those traits weren't part of her normal style.

Over a decade later, Sarah hired me as a consultant for a big event. During our planning meetings, I saw another side of her: she was concise, organized, and insightful. Our large group planning meetings were still jovial, but now they were also efficient and productive. One day Sarah and I went out to lunch and I admitted to her that I was suffering from debilitating insomnia since giving birth to my daughter. That's when she came clean; she told me that for all the years I worked for her, she slept perhaps four intermittent hours a night. Her brain was fried and she could barely hold it together. She said she didn't tell anyone because she feared that she'd highlight her behavior and "get caught" for poor performance. She told me that she valued me so much during that time because I helped her look good. Even if Sarah had confided in me during those years, I doubt I would have understood, because I had yet to learn just how much poor sleep compromises our brains.

I'm devoting a chapter to sleep because you can't live a truly brilliant life if you aren't sleeping well. Fortunately, there's much more awareness and acceptance that humans aren't robots, and can't be brilliant employees if they are exhausted. Books like *The Way We're Working Isn't Working* and Arianna Huffington's *The Sleep Revolution* have helped connect the science of sleep to overall effectiveness and health. Until recently, making do with very little sleep was something many people bragged about (as of writing this, Donald Trump is still proud of his 4.5 average hours of nightly sleep). Now, it's widely considered an indicator (leading or lagging) of burnout and diminished cognitive performance. In February, 2016, Nick van Dam and Els van der Helm authored a piece in the *Harvard Business*

Review, citing a McKinsey study of 189,000 people around the world that showed a clear connection between sleep and leadership effectiveness. Specifically, the HBR authors detail how poor sleep diminishes capacity in all of the following: decision-making, empathy, problem solving, inhibition, planning, and reasoning. Whether you want to be a more brilliant leader, parent, partner or performer of any kind, you must get adequate sleep.

While we've come a long way recently in our thinking about sleep, our institutions still lag. Employers can do more to encourage practices that help people prioritize sleep without falling behind in their work. And schools, particularly medical schools, can do a much better job of helping students and residents get more and better sleep. (I don't know about you, but I'd like my politicians, pilots, and doctors to get a good night's sleep every night.)

If you're one of the lucky few who prioritizes sleep, falls asleep easily, sleeps deeply, and wakes energized, feel free to skip this chapter. If, however, you are among the millions of people suffering from insomnia or poor sleep, you know how bad it sucks. So, please keep reading.

There are lots of books and articles out there about sleep and I highly encourage you to read them for more in-depth research. This chapter is different in a couple of ways. First, I'll keep the preaching short. Too many books seem to yell at the reader trying to convince them to sleep more, as if will is the only thing keeping them up at night. I know there are a few of you out there who think you can get by on less than seven hours, so I'll take a bit of time sharing the consequences of poor sleep with you. (If I don't convince you, please read *The Sleep Revolution* so she can properly inform and alarm you with research about how poor sleep is connected to diseases including cancer and Alzheimer's, and how poor sleep even makes us gain weight.) Also, many authors focus only on the mechanics of sleep: your environment and habits (also known as "sleep hygiene"). Since many of you already know what you're supposed to do, but haven't yet, you'll find a comprehensive sleep hygiene inventory later in this chapter. I encourage you to use it to make any necessary changes so you can give yourself an optimal chance at great sleep starting tonight. For those of you who know you need more sleep, and have tried changing your routine and environment but *still* can't sleep, I'm also focusing on *physiological* reasons you might not sleep well. By the end of this chapter, you'll have strategies for finding a medical professional who can properly diagnose and treat underlying causes—not just symptoms.

How Much Sleep is Enough?

I'd love to tell you that you can live brilliantly (or even get by) with less than seven hours of sleep, but the fact is, unless you're one of the five percent of humans who has a genetic mutation that permits you to thrive on less than seven hours, your brain desperately wants seven hours—minimum. Decide what time you need to wake, and then back up eight hours to determine your new bedtime. Experiment to see how you do with seven, eight, or nine hours.

I have one more bit of potentially annoying news: you're going to need to go to sleep by 10:00 PM. In his book, *Sleep Smarter*, Shawn Stevenson calls the period between 10:00 PM and 2:00 AM "money time" because your body produces the most melatonin and human growth hormone, also called the "youth hormone," during these hours. This may be why people who go to bed late wake up groggy despite getting eight hours of sleep. You may need to make some permanent changes to your evening routine, but it will prove worth it.

The High Cost of Poor Sleep

When I was a new mom, I felt as though I should have a warning sign in my car's back window that read, "Tired mom on board." A recent study conducted by the AAA Foundation for Traffic Safety confirmed my hunch that I had no business driving. They found that drowsy drivers are responsible for one in six—that's seventeen percent—of fatal car accidents. Poor sleep doesn't just affect your ability to drive (and your motor skills in general); it also wreaks havoc on your memory. Indeed, studies have shown that exhaustion produces the cognitive equivalent of drunkenness. A disrupted sleep cycle also adversely affects your body's production of melatonin, which is both a hormone and a potent antioxidant against cancer, thus raising your risk of breast cancer. Poor sleeping habits can also raise your levels of corticosterone, a stress hormone, making you quick to lash out at innocent and unsuspecting victims. Oh . . . and it causes premature aging. To sum up, poor sleep will cost you your brilliant potential.

That's the bad news. The good news is that, no matter how long you've struggled with sleep, you can get better.

MY BROKEN BRAIN

In 2007, I gave birth to my baby girl. My daughter was born healthy, aside from congenital hip dysplasia. She made chirping sounds from day one and earned the nickname "Cricket." Less than a week later, those sounds turned to screams—probably a result of painful colic and undiagnosed celiac disease. Fitted into a hip brace that splayed her legs, she would only sleep in my arms.

Thus began my sleep torture. I stayed up all night holding her. People would ask if I slept while she slept. Because of my hip and pelvis condition, the only way I can sleep is lying flat on my right side, with a pillow between my knees and a tennis ball under muscles damaged in the car accident. So I stayed awake and sat up in pain while my daughter got a few precious hours of sleep (and I got a few precious hours of quiet). We hired a night nurse, but at twenty-five dollars an hour, all we felt we could afford was a mere four hours for five nights. I got to sleep from 11:00 PM to 2:00 AM, then had to wake to relieve her.

I should have asked for more help; I knew I was a mess. But like a fish that doesn't know she's swimming in water, I didn't see my situation clearly. As it was my first child, I assumed this was normal, and I felt shame for not handling it well. I thought if I asked for help it would be an admission that I wasn't a capable mom. It wasn't until the doctors' diagnoses that I learned how extreme my situation was.

At about age four months, my daughter stopped screaming, lost the hip brace, and became her true happy, smiling, calm self. I thought, "*Now* I can sleep." But four months of only two or three hours of very light sleep per day had *fried my brain* (and adrenals). Consequently, I was unable to fall into a deep sleep or stay asleep for long. Nor could I nap, no matter how much I tried. This continued for many more months.

When I say that my mission is to help people go from burned out to brilliant, I know from experience what that feels like. It took me years to climb out of the hole. But I rebuilt my nervous, adrenal, and hormonal systems with the help of gifted doctors. Most of my clients (thankfully) are nowhere near as messed up as I was from sleep deprivation. But they're on their way. Little by little, they're damaging their health and using temporary "Band-Aid" treatments like caffeine and sleep aids.

If you're lucky, you can make changes to your environment and start sleeping better tonight, but it's quite possible that there are underlying biological conditions that are keeping you from sleeping soundly, regardless of how great your pre-bedtime routine and environment are.

Sleep Hygiene Best Practices

- **Go to bed and get up at the same time every day—even on the weekends.** This will help keep your biological clock in sync. People who sleep in on weekends tend to create a sense of jet lag in their bodies, as if they are travelling across time zones.
- **Develop a sleep ritual by doing the same things each night just before bed.** Parents often establish a routine for their kids, but it can help adults too. A routine cues the body to settle down for the night.

- **Don't drink any fluids within two hours of going to bed.** This will reduce the likelihood of needing to get up and go to the bathroom, or at least minimize the frequency. And go to the bathroom right before bed.

- **Eat a high-protein snack several hours before bed.** This can provide the L-tryptophan needed for your melatonin and serotonin production.

- **Avoid grain and sugar snacks before bed.** These will raise your blood sugar and delay sleep. Later, when your blood sugar drops too low (known as hypoglycemia), you may wake up and be unable to fall back asleep.

- **Take a hot bath, shower, or sauna before bed.** When your body temperature is raised in the late evening, it will fall at bedtime, facilitating sleep. The temperature drop from getting out of the bath signals to your body it's time for bed.

- **Avoid caffeine in the afternoon.** You'll need to experiment to learn your cutoff time. If you're going to bed at 10:00, you'll likely want to avoid caffeine after 1:00.

- **Avoid alcohol close to bedtime.** It tends to prevent your body from progressing to the deepest levels of REM sleep, and if you overindulge, may wake you up when the dehydrating effects kick in.

- **Keep the room dark.** It's important to sleep in as close to complete darkness as possible so you don't disturb your circadian rhythms. That said, it's not always easy to block out every stream of light using curtains, blinds, or drapes, particularly if you live in an urban area. In these cases, wear a comfortable eye mask.

- **Put your work away at least one hour before bed (preferably two hours or more).** This will give your mind a chance to unwind so you can go to sleep feeling calm, not hyped up or anxious about tomorrow's deadlines.

- **No TV right before bed**. Even better, get the TV out of the bedroom or even completely out of the house. It's too stimulating to the brain, preventing you from falling asleep quickly.

- **Read something spiritual or uplifting or boring.** This may help you relax. Don't read anything stimulating, such as a mystery or suspense novel, which has the opposite effect. In addition, if you're really enjoying a suspenseful book, you might be tempted to go on reading for hours instead of going to sleep!

- **If reading doesn't help, listen to boring audiobooks or recordings made specifically for sleep.** Some people also find the sound of white noise or nature sounds, such as the ocean or forest, soothing for sleep. Every night, I wear comfortable "SleepPhones" and listen to a program called "floating" that contains realistic ocean sounds with customized subliminal affirmations (undetectable in the background) created by Centerpointe.

- **Keep the room cool**. Between 60 and 68 degrees.

- **Sleep on a comfortable bed with breathable sheets.** Thread count isn't as important as material, and super high thread count (over 400) can actually cause your body to become too hot. I find that Pima cotton is most comfortable.

- **Dim the lights throughout the house in the evening.** Avoid looking at any lit devices before bed.

If you read on an iPad or similar device, read for *no more than an hour*, as the light affects your melatonin. I read on a Kindle Paperwhite, with an internal self-adjusting light that doesn't contain the blue rays that confuse your body into a wakeful state.

- **Go to bed with positive thoughts.** Write down a few things that you are grateful for in your life or in your day. Think about something good that happened today and let that sink in and fill you with pleasure. (Check out Rick Hanson's *Taking in the Good* practice that helps us savor/ruminate on positive experiences.)

- **Exercise regularly.** People who exercise a few times a week sleep better than people who don't. Don't exercise past 7:00 PM.

- **Lower stress by preparing for your morning.** Pack your purse or briefcase, prepare lunches and snacks, and have everyone in the family pack their backpacks and select their outfits for the next day, so your mind isn't tempted to worry about it.

- **Download stressful thoughts to paper.** If you find yourself too stressed to sleep, make a list of all the things you need to do. Keep a notebook by the bed so that if you wake up and find your mind is swirling, write down your thoughts without getting out of the bed.

- **If you wake in the night (and it's normal if you do) do not turn on anything with a light source.** Instead, find a comfortable position and try your own version of counting sheep. You might count breaths. I like to envision tulips passing through my imagination, each one a different color. I often touch my calm point (thumb to inner lower middle finger, between first and second knuckle) and do Andrew Weil's the 4-7-8 Breath technique (four counts in, hold for seven counts, eight counts out). I also keep Bach's Rescue Remedy (a homeopathic tincture) on my bedside table and spray it under my tongue if I wake up and worry about getting back to sleep. My daughter now uses Kids' Rescue Remedy. While reading the intense fifth Harry Potter book, we discovered that it worked wonders for calming her dream-filled mind so she could drift into to a peaceful sleep.

- **Experiment with clothing and temperature, especially socks.** Socks have a significant impact on body temperature. If you tend to get hot at night, try going sockless and/or leaving a foot out from the covers. I've found that lately, my body sleeps best with one sock on and one sock off.
- **Sleep alone.** That means kicking out the kids, pets, and even your partner. If you're a light sleeper, having another being in the room is almost guaranteed to disrupt your sleep. This doesn't mean that you can't have romance or snuggling! The whole family will feel the positive payoff when you start sleeping better.
- **Take melatonin drops before bed.** Be careful, though, as too much melatonin can make you groggy in the morning. I prefer drops so I can regulate how much I take in.
- **Reduce electromagnetic frequencies (EMFs).**
  - ○ Unplug all electrical devices in your bedroom while sleeping.

- Put your cell phone on "airplane mode," leave it in a different room, or turn it off altogether. The sound alone is enough to warrant turning it off.
- Avoid digital clocks on the bedside table.
- Mattresses with metal coiling may conduct electricity from other sources, exposing you to high levels of EMFs.

Physical Symptoms that Prevent Good Sleep

If you've done all you can to create the right conditions for sleep, but still can't sleep, it's time to consider biological factors and get proper help. If you've visited a healthcare practitioner but still can't sleep, don't despair. This section will guide you to someone who can actually cure you.

FINDING THE RIGHT DOCTOR

The most important tool you have in your quest for good sleep is a competent medical partner. I have so much admiration and empathy for medical professionals. But the sad truth is that most doctors may help you get from burnout to blah, but they likely won't help you return to your most brilliant nature. It's quite possible that you won't find a sleep expert on your insurance's preferred doctor list, as many traditional doctors aren't well equipped to cure sleep issues. I suspect it has to do with being so regulated by insurance that they can't run as many tests or spend the adequate intake time necessary to find the true causes. If you're reading this, then you've suffered long enough and need to find the right person fast. You need a relentless, curious, medical detective who wants to cure you, not put a Band-Aid over your symptoms.

The Mayo Clinic lists ten causes for insomnia, one of which is "health problems." That one cause alone could have fifty or more variations including sleep apnea, structural problems like back or leg pain, hormonal issues, neurotransmitter problems, or endocrine imbalances. My insomnia was caused by weakened adrenals, anxious thoughts, low vitamin D, hormonal imbalances, and an inability to absorb folic acid (and a partridge in a pear tree!).

You want a doctor who accepts that insomnia is a complex problem that rarely has a simple solution. You need a medical detective who doesn't get scared off by complexity—someone who's willing to investigate and rule out possibilities until they solve the riddle, who has enough experience to draw upon, yet doesn't try to quickly lump you into a simple category and send you on your way. If you've been working with a doctor for some time and don't seem to be getting better, it may be time to move on. It may be that you and your doctor have different definitions of "cured."

By the time I sought out help, I was a mess. I found a competent professional who helped me get a little better, but I reached a plateau with her. When she retired I was forced to find someone new. One day I was listening to a teleconference where Dr. Morgan Camp talked about helping executives regain optimal health. I decided to seek him out for my own problems even though he wasn't in my insurance network. He reviewed my records, talked with me at length, and offered an idea. Traditional saliva tests measure your cortisol levels at four points during waking hours. On a hunch, he had me do one more saliva test during one of my middle-of-the-night awakenings. Sure enough, he found that my cortisol was spiking in the middle of the night. No wonder I couldn't get back to sleep despite all the best sleep hygiene habits. My body had adapted to the needs of a baby born with congenital problems. After four months of waking at 2:00 AM and staying awake with a crying baby, my body adapted. As soon as we got the results, I began taking a pill at bedtime that lowered my cortisol to normal levels, then another in the morning that boosted my weakened adrenals. That simple thing would eliminate one of my nighttime wakeups and helped me return to sleep.

While it seems natural now that he would make this modification to the test, it was an incredibly creative solution; nowhere in the test instructions did it recommend such a deviation from the traditional schedule. My sleep got much better until years later when it got very bad again. I was about to get divorced and had moved into a new home. Most people just assumed my sleep was bad because of stress. But that didn't feel right. And I had other peculiar symptoms like shortness of breath and intolerance for exercise. I went back to my doctor, who listened carefully and had me do another series of lab and in-house tests. We learned that I had a genetic mutation that that kept me from absorbing folic acid. Little did I know that while I was trying to do the right thing during my pregnancy by taking folic acid supplements, I was actually poisoning myself. My body was completely out of whack from something that doesn't even show up on the common list of causes of insomnia! Only a doctor with determination and curiosity could have figured this out. A true medical detective will run extensive tests—blood, urine, saliva— in search of all possible clues. If your doctor is unwilling to do extensive testing, it's a sign that he's either lazy, burned-out, incompetent, or all of the above.

QUICK FIXES DON'T FIX

If your doctor prescribes a sleeping pill, it's a possible sign that he or she isn't up for solving the mystery. Insomnia is a symptom of an underlying problem. A little pill is not going to solve the underlying problem. It may mask symptoms for a while but the problem will persist and probably grow, leaving you feeling worse than when you started. Plus, while sleeping pills may seem to help, they actually prevent you from getting deep sleep. Instead, they put you into a light sleep state, which may leave you feeling groggy in the morning. Your condition may end up requiring medications to address certain imbalances. While sleeping pills never helped me sleep, Xanax (for PTSD) did. But it took me many months to sleep without it. The idea is to get targeted solutions that restore balance so your body can fall asleep naturally and sleep deeply, and you can be your most brilliant, energized, well-rested self. If your doctor only uses drugs as a temporary relief while working to understand the underlying issues better, consider keeping her, but ask more questions and don't give up until you're sleeping without prescription pills.

Positivity and Sleep

If your poor sleep isn't caused by physical or environmental factors, you're likely to get great results if you work on lowering anxiety and increasing positivity. As you probably know, this is easier said than done, especially when your brain is sleep deprived. University of Notre Dame professor Jessica Payne showed a direct link between sleep, stress, and positivity. She also found that the easiest of the three to improve was positivity. But "easy" is a relative term; we could all use a little help battling our brains' natural negativity bias. I give all my clients this wonderfully simple and effective crutch—a free app designed with the help of neuroscientists called "e-Catch the Feeling." Playing this deceptively simple game will help increase your positive thoughts and lower the frequency of negative thoughts in just a few weeks. As with all technology, I recommend playing this game during daylight hours. I have my clients and workshop participants download the app while I'm there, so it doesn't slip their mind. I suggest you take a moment to download it now, and even play a few quick rounds before you read another page. Play the app for a few minutes a day for three weeks, and you'll have new wiring for greater positivity, which will positively impact stress and sleep.

REFLECTION QUESTIONS

On a scale of 1–10, how well are you sleeping? (This is, of course, a relative measure, but 1 would be about as bad as possible and 10 represents sleeping through the night, waking naturally and well-rested.)

If you answered 6 or lower, answer the following:

- What consequences are you currently experiencing from poor sleep?

- What action step(s) will you try tonight from the sleep hygiene list? (If you're feeling ambitious, implement several and then if you like, take away one at a time to see which have the greatest impact.)

- What next step will you take toward finding the right practitioner to help?

PART TWO:

HOW?

CHAPTER SEVEN:

How *Not* to Change

I'm an expert at weight loss ... I've done it fifty times.
—ANONYMOUS

Congratulations. The fact that you've read this far tells me a lot about you and gives me great confidence that you won't just *read* this book, but will actually *apply the teachings* to step closer to your brilliant potential.

Michelle was a participant in my group-coaching program. She was an individual contributor in the program management office of a large marketing department in a multibillion-dollar company. She wanted to learn how to better influence others, given that her role created a sense in some people that she was inserting processes that slowed them down and stymied their independence. After our first meeting, where she learned that the program could help her improve *any* aspect of her performance and well-being, she admitted to the group that her deepest desire was to lose weight so she could look and feel better for her son's wedding in five months' time. For weeks, while the other five members of the group reported personal and professional successes, Michelle had little to say about her personal goal. She told us that she just couldn't get motivated to change. Then, a couple months into the program, something shifted when she went dress shopping, and she decided that she *had* to change. Then, using the system I'll outline in Chapter Nine, she rearranged her schedule and got the right support. Two months later, at the end of our program, she'd lost fifteen pounds. I ran into her in the hallway a couple months later and I barely recognized her. She was confident, happy, and at least three sizes smaller, beaming as she showed me photos of her son's wedding.

If you've ever been passionately determined to achieve a goal—and then failed to achieve it—you know how hard it is to change habits. I'm guessing that despite your many successes, you beat yourself up on a semi-regular basis for letting yourself down in areas that matter to you—areas that are important, but not urgent. Unfortunately, no amount of shame or guilt will help you achieve a goal. If that were the case, we'd all be happy, fit, fulfilled, and rich.

In this chapter, I'll show you the most common mistakes people make when trying to achieve a goal, and how to overcome them.

Why Change is Hard

While I'm not letting you off the hook, I do want to assure you that it's really not your fault that you haven't achieved everything on your wish list. That's because the biological cards are stacked against you. You see, your safety-seeking brain doesn't really want you to change—even when that change is good for you. To your brain, any change equals pain. And your brain (which, as you already know, is running on a nearly unchanged hundred-thousand-year-old operating system) would rather see you fat, tired, addicted, and/or distracted, than endure any habit change.

That's because the brain has just one mission: to keep you safe and alive. And your brain defines safety as moving you toward pleasure and away from pain. To your brain, habit change is pure pain. For example, if you smoke cigarettes, your brain wants you to keep smoking. Stressful day at work? Your brain says, "Have another chip, bowl of ice cream, or glass of wine just like we always do! We'll feel better!" There's good news though; you can trick your brain. And if you want to go from burned out (or blah) to brilliant, you must. You can achieve any goal once you stop making the three most common mistakes that sabotage you every time. Let's start with the biggest, most common self-sabotaging mistake:

TOO MUCH, TOO FAST

The biggest mistake people make when they set out to achieve something is to make the first step too ... BIG.

When you set an audacious goal like "I'm going to lose two dress sizes in two months" or "I'm going to go from sedentary to marathon in six months," your brain puts the brakes on and does all it can to foil your plans. It's like your brain says, "Are you nuts? Why on earth would you want to do such a crazy thing? That's not who we are!" It's not that you can't set and achieve audacious goals, but how you go about it has to change. You have to eat the elephant

one . . .

bite . . .

at . . .

a . . .

time.

(My apologies to majestic elephants.)

While massive change requires massive action, you can't start with massive action and hope to sustain it. You have to take your goal and break it down into small steps. Then you break it down again until you find the smallest incremental change you can make. How can you tell it's the right size? Well, it will probably feel pathetically inadequate. As author James Altucher writes in his best-selling book *Choose Yourself*, if you want to become a person who flosses her teeth, start by flossing *one tooth*. Your brain will start to reprogram itself to recognize "Hey, this isn't so bad. I'm actually a person who flosses." Then it becomes easier and in fact, natural, to increase the goal. In time, your brain will redefine flossing from pain to pleasure. You'll have tricked and retrained your brain.

You may have experienced this with exercise. Once your brain begins to identify movement with pleasure, *not* exercising becomes painful. Your brain (and body) will begin to crave the new behavior and the associated endorphins, helping you turn it into a habit.

Another good sign that the mini-goal is right-sized is that you can take that step today, if not right now. So, a goal of exercising six days a week might begin with a five-minute walk as soon as you finish this sentence.

The moment you take any action, you begin to build momentum. Over time, you can increase the activity. So, go ahead: make that appointment for the mammogram or colonoscopy; call that friend or family member; block off vacation time on your calendar; buy a blender—just take one baby step toward your goal.

Whatever you do will be insignificant, but it is very important that you do it.

—Mahatma Gandhi

Then notice that you feel a little lighter, a little less guilty, and more confident.

CHOOSING THE WRONG GOAL

Too often, we choose to work on things because we think we *should* based on what outside influencers (family, friends, *Cosmo* magazine, etc.) tell us, instead of what our heart and soul most deeply craves. This is why in the next chapter I will ask you to complete the Brilliant Life Assessment.

At a recent talk I gave entitled "How to Say No With Grace, Not Guilt," one participant shared that he came into the workshop believing that his primary goal should be to eat better. Clearly, this is a worthy endeavor. But when he did the Brilliant Life Assessment exercise, he discovered that the biggest and most painful gap concerned his connection to his immediate family. He felt a huge sense of clarity and urgency because his wife and children were so important to him, yet he'd neglected to nurture those relationships. When I asked what he was going to do about it—what mini-step he would take— he said he'd already texted his wife that he wanted to take the family out to dinner, where he'd share his new commitment and ask for their ideas.

RELYING ON WILLPOWER

Imagine that you've started a diet and are committed to eating only healthy food. You're doing great until 2:00 PM rolls around and you realize that you've skipped lunch and now have to go to your next meeting famished, "hangry," and distracted by your rumbling stomach and under-fueled brain. One thoughtful (and evil) colleague brings a box of gooey chocolate chunk cookies to the meeting. What do you do? Willpower is, from a neurological perspective, nearly nonexistent. Your brain wants to do what's habitual, not necessarily what's good for you or what you promised yourself you would do. And when your brain is tired, hungry, stressed, distracted, or doing something unfamiliar, it's even less likely to stick with the plan.

Now you know why you've failed to live up to your desire to change. It's not because you're weak, or unmotivated, or incapable: it's because you're human. Now that you know what *not* to do, let's learn how to choose a realistic goal.

CHAPTER EIGHT:

How to Choose the Right Goal

*Choosing how we spend our time
is the hardest decision we make.*

—TONY ROBBINS, *Ultimate Edge* Audio Program

So far, I've given you a lot of possible areas to improve upon, including positivity, sleep, and managing technology. Hopefully you're feeling more inspired than overwhelmed, but if you're daunted by all the possible things you could do to improve your life, this short chapter will help you get clear and focused; I'm about to make it easier than you ever believed possible to find the right focus, overcome obstacles, and take steps to redirect the ship away from burnout and toward brilliance.

When it comes to self-development, one of the hardest things to do is to decide where to invest your precious time and energy. In this chapter, I'll help you pick *one* goal worthy of your time and energy.

Recognizing Your *Shoulds*

As I mentioned earlier, the human brain is only motivated by the desire to feel pleasure and avoid pain. And it turns out that pain is a bigger motivator than pleasure. Kind of makes sense when you think about it: if you place your hand on a hot burner, you're going to pull it away instantly. So, if you want to achieve a goal, you'd better pick an area of focus so painful that you can no longer stand it.

If you truly want to lose weight, for example, go to a Macy's dressing room, try on swimsuits, and look at your butt in the three-way mirror under florescent lighting. If you don't feel extreme pain from this exercise, you probably picked the wrong goal.

Here's another way to tell if your goal is wrong. Do you describe it as something that you "should" do? As in, "I *should* really eat better," or, "I *should* really be more present with my kids," or, "I *should* really get more sleep," or, "I *should* get off my butt and exercise." Here's the big problem with *shoulds:* they don't get done. The only thing *shoulds* do is make you feel guilty and pathetic for not taking action. They cause pain, but not in a way that motivates you to do anything about it.

Let me share some *shoulds* that have spent time on my list:

- I should drink less wine.
- I should lose a few pounds.
- I should practice speaking French instead of wasting my degree.
- I should be speaking on stage with the best of the best.

- I should be more patient and less distracted with my daughter.
- I should blog more often.
- I should e-mail my list more often.
- I should practice the cello.
- I should give Amazon.com less money.
- I should do yoga.
- I should spend more time with friends and less time working.
- I should do more marketing.
- I should schedule a checkup with my primary care doctor.
- I should talk to a financial advisor.
- I should put all my programs in an online version that people can access anywhere, anytime.
- I should call the dentist.
- I should save more money.
- I should finish this frickin' book.

Ick.

Go ahead and make a list of all the *shoulds* you tell yourself on a regular basis. Have fun with it; write freely and without judgment. If you're reading this as an e-book, grab whatever piece of paper is nearby and start scribbling.

I regularly tell myself that I should:

_____

_____

_____

_____

_____

_____

_____

_____

_____

_____

If you now feel like crap, then you did this exercise well. (I promise we'll take care of your toxic *shoulds* in the next chapter.) None of those items are likely to happen unless you upgrade them from a wimpy *should,* to a powerful *must.* We inhale and exhale because we *must.* Our heart beats because it *must.* You take your kid to school every day and show up at work every day because you *must.* We don't say things like "I should really start blinking my eyes." Our lives won't end if we don't take time to spend with friends, build a deeply loving relationship with our partner, or spend quality time with our kids. But gradually, and then suddenly, we wake up and realize that we've squandered precious days, relationships, and potential.

So how do you decide which *should* to upgrade?

Your Brilliant Life Assessment

The critical next step in choosing the right goal requires you to take two minutes to visit my website and download my Brilliant Life Assessment that I give my new clients and workshop participants. My clients are amazed at how clear they get in just a few minutes when using this tool. This simple tool helps you tap into your subconscious awareness and discover your deepest desire. Don't be tempted to continue reading without doing the assessment! Right now, your brain is annoyed that you're even thinking of making it shift gears and go get the tool. Be the boss of your brain. And when it's tempted to open e-mail or social media, take charge and just go here: www.brillianceinc.com/resources. Also, tell your brain it's no big deal and in less than ten minutes, you (and your brain) will have some amazingly helpful information that will help you decimate that awful "should list" that you just created.

Here's an abbreviated version of the Assessment:

BRILLIANT LIFE ASSESSMENT INSTRUCTIONS

1. Draw a dot or "v" at the numerical level that represents how much you *value* each of the elements along the bottom.
2. Connect the dots with lines, forming one mountain range.
3. Draw an "x" or "s" at the numerical level that represents how *satisfied* you are with this element.
4. Connect them so you have a second mountain range.

5. Notice where you have something that feels like a relatively high value (e.g. 7 or higher), and where you have a significant satisfaction gap (e.g. 3 or more). This is not a scientific process so feel free to go with your gut when deciding which gap is the most painful.

6. Circle the *one* element that has the most painful gap

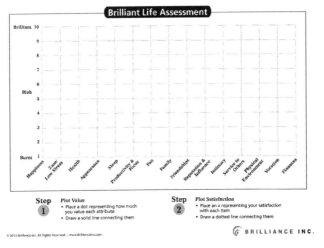

Larger version available at www.BrillianceInc.com/Resources

If you have more than one element with a painful gap, pick *one* that you can't stand any longer: one that's causing you so much pain that you *must* do it. Or, identify one that would cause you immense pleasure if you achieved it. Or, pick the one that will positively affect other parts of your life. For example, exercise will help you feel less stressed, sleep better, have more energy, look better, and think more clearly and creatively. And all that will help you have more capacity for relationships.

If you still have trouble deciding, you might pick one that has to get done before the others can. For example, if you're not sleeping well, prioritize that because without enough sleep, you won't have the mental and emotional capacity to undertake other goals.

You don't have to know *how* you're going to achieve it. You don't even have to believe it's possible to achieve. I promise we'll get to that in the next chapter. For now, you just have to know that it's so painful that you can no longer settle for the status quo: it's become intolerable and non-negotiable. Write it in the space below:

I *must* _____

_____

Once you upgrade a "should do" to a "must do," you'll find a way to make it happen.

> *Leap and the net will appear.*
> —John Burroughs

Where to Stuff Your *Shoulds*

Now, I want you to go back to your craptastic list of *shoulds* from the beginning of this chapter. If you skipped it, I encourage you to do it now so you can benefit from this next simple exercise. Do you see your new, upgraded *must* on the list? If so, circle it (and if you like, draw happy faces, stars, or hearts around it) to let it know you're going to be paying some awesome attention to it.

Now for the rest of the list.

Please take a moment to cross out every other item on your list. (If you like, you can draw daggers, flames, blood, or anything else that feels satisfying.) If you're worried that this means you'll never improve those items, don't fear.

One giant caveat to this second part of the exercise: I've said that I want you to upgrade only one *should* on your list, and drop your focus on other goals while you work on the most important one. However, some things are non-negotiable in my mind. If you're not sleeping well, make sure you've read the chapter on sleep and are prepared to take action to get a minimum of seven quality hours of sleep a night. And if visiting a doctor or dentist for routine tests is on your *should do* list, and you haven't seen one in the last year, upgrade those as well; if you haven't had a physical, mammogram, blood panel, colonoscopy, or other basic medical assessment, make that a priority. Just frickin' do it.

Two years ago, I was working with a client who had a big high-pressure job and travelled almost constantly. He didn't eat great or get regular exercise but still he slept well and had great stamina. One day he didn't show up for our call. Then he didn't respond to e-mail. Time went by and I reached out to his assistant who told me he was on medical leave but didn't share details. Finally, over two months later he called. He'd suffered a heart attack. When they drew blood in the hospital, it was too syrupy to even test. He didn't know that diabetes ran in his family (a great-grandfather had passed at a young age from it) and had neglected to get a physical in years.

He was forty-one, a husband and father, and he narrowly escaped death. He got a lucky second chance and within four months of the incident, after overhauling his diet, schedule, and exercise routine, he was no longer diabetic and went down from six medications to just one.

Most of us only change when we've had a catastrophic wakeup call in our health, relationships, or career. I want you to course-correct before it's too late. Ironically, this morning I received my blood test results from my Kaiser Permanente doctor via e-mail. We took the test mainly to assess my thyroid, since I—like my mother and grandmother—have hypothyroidism. I learned, to my shock, that I am just on the cusp of prediabetic. The irony is that I consume almost zero sugar (not even via fruit or grains) and exercise at least forty-five minutes a day. My diet consists of vegetables, proteins, nuts, and one fruit: avocado. I would never, ever have suspected it. Another doctor—my insanely gifted chiropractor/shaman Lisa Koenig—found that for some reason, my body is not metabolizing the little sugar I consume. Fortunately, she got it jump-started again in one visit. My point in sharing this is, regardless of the goal you've chosen to upgrade, make getting a health snapshot a must.

As to the remainder of the *should* list, don't panic as you demote items. When you cross things off your should list, all you're saying is:

*This is not the time for me to use
my limited capacity to improve this.
I'm dropping the guilt
and taking this off my list . . . for now.*

You can always revisit it when you have more capacity.

As I mentioned in the Introduction to this book, I know something about limited capacity. My path to where I am today has been bumpy and full of physical hurdles that slowed my desired pace of progress. For example, in 2011 I hired a high-performance coach to help me achieve some big personal and business goals. It was going well until, with about two months left in the program, my husband and I decided that our fifteen-year marriage was over in all manner but legal. Suddenly, my priorities shifted and I had to funnel all my energy into transitioning my daughter to kindergarten while prepping a house for sale, finding a new place to live, moving, and going through divorce mediation. I can't convey how debilitating it was emotionally, but if you've been there, you know. Making this huge life transition as gracefully as possible was my new *must*. Everything else was on the back burner.

Then, a few months later, when I was settled in to a new place and thought I could move some business goals into the *must* column, I was hit with a mysterious illness characterized by labored breathing, debilitating fatigue, mental fog, and anxiety. Six months later, after many hours in blood labs, I was diagnosed with mold poisoning and Lyme disease (two for the price of one!). Regaining my health and eradicating the mold source became my *musts*. Until I had better health and vitality, I couldn't address the other items on my list.

There's no shame in recognizing your limited capacity. In fact, admitting and honoring your limitations without guilt takes courage and strength.

Making Space for Your New Goal

In the next chapter, you'll learn my simple, six-step process for achieving your goal. And in Chapter Ten, you'll learn how to decline requests with grace, not guilt, so you can focus your precious energies in the right place.

REFLECTION QUESTIONS

1. What's important to you about your new *must*?

2. If you don't improve it, what pain will it cause?

3. If you do improve it, what pleasure will you gain?

CHAPTER NINE:

How to Change for Good

*The most common mistake that people make is
setting their sights on an event, a transformation,
an overnight success they want to achieve—rather
than focusing on their habits and routines.*

—JAMES CLEAR, *Transform Your Habits*

In Chapter Seven you learned the universal traps we all
fall into when trying to change habits. Then you identified
a realistic, achievable, meaningful goal using the Brilliant
Life Assessment. Now, I'll share the proven six-step
process I use to help my clients (and myself) achieve
goals that have been bugging them for ages. While I'll
use weight loss as one example, the process I outline here
will help you achieve *any* goal. Unless you want to fail a
million times daily, you must do these six things:

1. Create an inspiring vision

2. Get support

3. Create schedules, reminders, and rituals

4. Remove temptation

5. Reward yourself

6. Upgrade your identity

Let's look at each of them more closely.

Create an Inspiring Vision

Once you've turned your *should do* into a *must do*, you're ready to turn it into an "I will" by creating an inspiring vision. Let's work with a diet example since many of us can relate to it. Most of us focus on goals more than vision, as in: "I'll lose two swimsuit sizes before Memorial Day." Maybe you've been taught that in order to achieve greatness, you have to create a goal that follows the SMART model (Specific, Measurable, Achievable, Realistic, Time-bound).

One problem with SMART goals is that when we set a specific time frame for achieving a goal, we can get tunnel vision and forget that new habits are formed through small daily actions. We can control our daily actions, but we can't control how long it will take us to achieve our goal. For example, two people on the same diet may both have a goal of losing weight by May 31, but their unique bodies will achieve that goal at different paces. When we set up rigid time-bound goals, we're setting ourselves up for disappointment when we don't achieve it. Thinking back to Michelle, whom we met in Chapter Seven, while her goal was about losing weight in time for a wedding, I helped her frame it not as a number, but as a feeling—one of confidence and pride.

If you truly want to motivate yourself, create a vision, not a target. Here are a few examples of visions worth working for:

- Strong and healthy
- Calm and happy
- Joyful, connected family life
- Freedom to work where, when, and with whom you want
- Sleeping deeply every night, waking rested with enough capacity to do all you're called to do and want to do
- Becoming a leader who inspires others to greatness and is widely admired
- Ending each day with a sense of completion and achievement

Look back at your new *must do*. Close your eyes (after you've read this paragraph!) and really imagine that you've accomplished it. Maybe you're wearing a size you've dreamed of for years. Or, maybe you envision a new website launched, or your book on the best-seller list. Imagine yourself on the other side of this challenge. What do you feel? What is different about your life? How do you feel about yourself?

Go ahead and envision . . .

Is your vision so compelling that you'll do anything to make it real? Can you sense the immense pleasure (or reduced pain) that will accompany the achievement? Please don't worry yet about *how* you're going to achieve the vision. We'll talk more about planning soon.

A word of caution about creating a personal vision:

It's tempting to compare yourself to others or to your ideal vision of where you *should* be. Be honest about your current state and honor your unique path and circumstances. For example, before I could even begin to lose weight, I had to work with my holistic MD, Dr. Morgan Camp in Mill Valley, California, to repair the damage to my endocrine system after a difficult childbirth and post-birth. Without balanced adrenals, hormones, and thyroid, I wouldn't have been able to effectively address my weight and strength goals—no wonder I hit a plateau in my weight loss. And before writing a book, I had to reverse symptoms from mold poisoning and Lyme disease, which I did with holistic MD Dr. Raj Patel in Redwood City, California.

Once you have a compelling vision worth striving for, you'll need to gather support and create structures to help make the vision real.

Get Support

An inspiring, motivating vision is simply not enough. Failure to stick with your plan isn't a sign of weakness; it's normal. Psychologists Piercarlo Valdesolo and David DeSteno have shown that we actually have two selves they call present-self and future-self. Present-you sets goals and believes that you will be able to resist temptation. But future-you can't always be trusted to do the noble thing. DeSteno writes that "While today you feel confident that you'll be able to honor your planned monthly contribution to your retirement savings, window shopping at the Apple Store next week may change all that. The result? A broken promise to yourself." Remember that evil cookie-pushing colleague in Chapter Seven? Future-you will likely eat the cookie if the right support isn't in place. Then present-you will beat yourself up.

You can guard against your undependable future-you by creating systems of support: technical support in the form of diet or exercise apps, for example, or human support like coaches, trainers, nutritionists or financial planners. If you don't gather the right support for you and your particular vision, you're likely to end up annoyed and dejected that you didn't achieve your goal . . . again. Everyone needs support. Even coaches have coaches. At any point in time, I have at least one person supporting me. Depending on the goal and problems, I have a spiritual coach, life coach, financial planner, business coach, chiropractor, massage therapist, holistic MD, traditional MD, friends, and colleagues. Books like this one (and the myriad other self-help books on your bookshelf or e-reader) are great for spurring change and providing structures, but they can't replace the magic that happens when you say your vision and commitment aloud to another human being.

Create Schedules, Reminders, and Rituals

If you wait for motivation to kick in, or if you tell yourself that you'll get to the new thing when you have time, you're unlikely to ever achieve your vision. Because your brain will be trying to thwart your change efforts, you need to set up an environment that supports you and helps you overcome inertia.

One of the first things I do with a client after they choose a development focus is review their schedule and figure out how and where to fit the new activity in. And if you're like me and nearly everyone I know, that alone can feel daunting. Most people think they can't possibly fit something else in. Even going to bed earlier can seem impossible. In the next chapter, you'll learn how to make space for your new habits.

Once you have space, you need to create an environment that allows you to do this painful thing (i.e., change) with relative ease. One of my clients, John, wanted to exercise more and sit less. He had a long commute and was on the road early, returning home late. He decided that he would take a thirty-minute run at 2:00 PM, when his body (and brain) needed an energy boost. He'd make up the time by staying later at work, which would help him miss rush-hour traffic. As you can imagine, this wasn't easy to stick with, so he made it easier by invoking support. His assistant blocked the time on his calendar. He told his team what he was up to and they gave him their full support. He bought sneakers and extra clothes and kept them in the locker room at the office. After a few days, he felt such a reward in terms of energy and mood boost that he now craved the run and would do all he could not to miss it. Rather than miss a day, he learned to do some kind of activity during this time, even if it meant having a walking meeting with a colleague.

Putting the event on the schedule isn't enough; it's too easy to forget to do it. We need reminders, or "cues" as Charles Duhigg calls them in his book, *The Power of Habit*. Author and bodybuilder James Clear offers a great activity for helping you build reminders into your

day. Make a list of things that you do without fail daily. For example:
- turn off alarm clock
- brush teeth
- get dressed
- drive
- eat
- look at phone
- open laptop
- read e-mail
- wash hands
- walk into a room
- open fridge
- shower
- go to bed

Any of these actions can act as reminders. For example, when I was trying to change a thought pattern, I repeated an affirmation every time I washed my hands or flushed a toilet (not glamorous, but it worked and added a touch of humor to my intention). If you're working on moving your body more, you might make yourself do as many push-ups or sit-ups as you can before you let yourself brush your teeth.

When I decided to learn to play cello, I made sure that the cello was out of its case, visible in the corner of the living room. My reminder to practice was connected to walking into the room. Note: I've not set a big audacious goal to give a concert by a certain date. Rather, my goal is to never miss a day of practice. And here's the interesting and wonderful thing about taking up a musical instrument: the reward is almost immediate. If you practice the same piece of music even for a short time every day, your brain builds new neural pathways so quickly that you feel and see improvement almost immediately. This improvement becomes almost addictive. The reward makes you want to practice even more.

An even better example of this near-immediate gratification is weight lifting. If done well, you'll likely feel some muscle pain. Even that will feel like a reward because it will be a reminder that your body is now repairing itself with stronger muscle fibers. When you return to the workout a few days later, you may find that you can do an extra rep. While weight loss can take a frustratingly long time to be visible, weight lifting provides tangible rewards. And the stronger you get, the more efficiently your body burns fat. Weight lifting will help you build confidence and improve your appearance, strength, and health by strengthening tissue and bones. If you're having trouble choosing a goal, you could do worse than to start there.

Some people might need a gym membership for their ritual. For me, a gym will actually demotivate me. Because I know I need fast and convenient exercise, I keep adjustable weights in my basement that take up nearly no space. I lift only three days a week for ten (or fewer) minutes at a time. But I work to muscle failure (the point at which you can no longer lift), which doesn't take long if you lift the right amount. I have more muscle definition now than I've ever had, and the associated rewards have made me addicted: new habit achieved.

For my clients who want to be less wedded to their smartphones and more present with their loved ones, I have them schedule fifteen minutes a night where they turn off the electronics and practice asking open-ended questions and listening. After a few days, if not sooner, they feel rewarded by the connection they create and by the positive reaction from their loved ones. After a while, they're able to increase the amount of time offline without withdrawal symptoms.

Another way to find good reminders is to make a second list of things that happen to you every day. Then pick one or two to act as cues. For example, if you're working on lowering your stress, you could choose to do a breathing exercise at every red light. Or, when your TV show ends or a commercial comes on, you could do plank position (for core strength) or push-ups. And if you're like me and never see a commercial because you record everything, you could do lunges and crunches during the show. For someone who schedules a run every morning upon waking, your reminder could be the alarm going off an hour early, and your ritual may involve putting on and lacing up your running shoes before your feet touch the ground. For me, waking is a cue to breathe for five minutes with the MyCalmBeat app.

Remove Temptation

Reminders, structures, and rituals help, but they aren't enough to keep your brain from pulling you back to the dark (and oh-so-comfortable) side. Anticipate that you'll have weak moments and remove the temptations that are too easily available. For example, if you decide to lose weight, you must: remove the tempting foods from your house; fill your kitchen with the right kinds of food; shop for groceries when you're not hungry; avoid the places where you normally indulge; and decline dinner requests or bring your own food to events until you've achieved your goal and built new habits. If you live with someone, recruit his or her help. Have them eat what you eat or, as one of my brilliant clients did, have them hide the cookies. You can't always avoid temptation, but you can set yourself up to make it easier to resist. Or, if you want to focus on one big task, remove temptation by closing all non-relevant screens, closing your door, and turning your phone on *do not disturb* or off (the only reason to keep it on might be to set an alarm for the duration you'd like to focus). In meetings (or with loved ones), remove the temptation for distraction by leaving your phone behind or turning it off.

One of my clients wanted to lose weight and feel less tired. She decided to start drinking green smoothies and reduce her carb and sugar intake. Her first baby steps included buying a blender and searching the Internet for recipes. In the early days of her habit formation, she had a three-day business conference. Losing weight and eating healthy was a must for her, so she had to figure out how to make it through these three days without losing ground. If you've ever been to one of these events, you know that you're constantly bombarded by decadent choices: pastries, pasta, sandwiches, cookies, brownies, sodas, and wine. Not to mention sitting on your butt all day. Pure toxicity. Rather than rely on pathetic willpower, she lugged her blender and a cooler of vegetables to her hotel room. While others were dragging, she was full of energy. She was one hundred percent committed to her new habit, so she found a way. She recently told me that she's addicted to green smoothies: new habit achieved.

Expect that you will get hungry at work. Pack a healthy lunch so you never skip it, and stash nuts in your desk drawer for a quick, healthy snack. You can even keep a bag of small dark chocolates handy. Make your brain happy (and more willing to let you change) by making it as easy as possible to follow your plan.

Reward Yourself

Give your pleasure-seeking brain something that makes it happy or you'll be compelled to pick up the old habit. So, if you've decided to exercise, you better pick something that brings you joy. As I mentioned, I hate gyms, but I love being outside, so I walk or hike in the beautiful area I'm lucky to call home.

If you're removing foods from your diet, what foods can you introduce that delight your senses? When I was removing sugar from my diet, I added stevia to coffee and flavored sparkling water to make it guilt-free delicious. Those are great, but I also sometimes reward myself in the evening with an incredible sipping tequila and a good book (or a savory decaf tea . . . but the tequila is more rewarding). What intrinsic reward do you get from your new behaviors? Confidence? Fitting into an old size? Envision and savor this reward.

Upgrade Your Identity

Who do you think you are? Really . . . I wanna know. Most of us don't think about this question, but we all have an identity story running in our subconscious. In order to achieve your vision, you're going to need a new, improved identity.

When changing habits, it's wise to align your identity story with the person you're trying to become. For example, if you want to get in shape, identify yourself as a *person who moves her body every day*. If you want to stop smoking, tell yourself that *you're a non-smoker*. If you want to be a great leader, identify as *someone who is patient, and delegates for the sake of growing others*. This identity—or "Horizon Point" as author Sharon Melnick calls it—will make it easier to choose the behavior that you're trying to embed as a habit. Then, when you inevitably fall of the wagon, the old habit will feel like an anomaly that's out of sync with who you are, and you'll likely do better next time.

I use this technique with all my executive clients. Early on I ask them how they want to be known. What legacy do they want to leave? What do they want people to say about them when they are out of earshot? Then we encapsulate it in an easy-to-remember, catchy, inspiring phrase. Recent examples include:

- Powerful force for good
- Fun, compassionate, sage
- Caring, empowering leader who helps others grow
- Calm, balanced leader who inspires others to live fully

TAME YOUR SUBCONSCIOUS IDENTITY

Our identity story acts as a powerful guide. The problem is, we all have a second, more powerful, *unintentional identity story* that will sabotage your good intentions if you don't recognize and tame it. We began crafting this accidental identity story at a young age as a coping response to a painful world. Whatever identity we developed, it was built to protect us from emotional hurt, which neurologically speaking, is worse than physical pain.

Some examples of hidden/subconscious stories include: extrovert, introvert, perfectionist, easygoing, optimist, realist, rebel, rule-follower, active, lazy, serious, lighthearted, to name a few.

These identities (you may have several) reside deep in our subconscious and shape our actions. (I use the word "subconscious" here, as it's more familiar than the term "non-conscious," which neuroscientists use to describe the vast majority of brain processes that occur beneath our awareness.) Someone who identifies as a slacker will take pride in avoiding the rat race and trappings of success. A perfectionist will spend inordinate time making sure the details are just right so no one—including herself—can find fault. Someone who identifies as fat or lazy is unlikely to eat right or exercise, because in her mind, "Why bother? It's not going to make a difference." Unless you name it and tame it, your subconscious identity will fuel actions that will eventually damage your spirit, results, health, and relationships, until one day you wake up feeling incomplete, painfully discovering that you've led an unnecessarily small life.

I see this play out with my clients. Pam was recently promoted to vice president. She cares deeply about her people and wants very much to improve her health and spend more quality time with her family. Yet Pam is fiercely and subconsciously committed to preserving the identity that has worked for her all these years and propelled her to success. So, despite her good intentions, her control freak, perfectionist self stays late working on projects that she could have delegated, or that were good enough a week ago. She dwells on small details and feels a sense of pride in her work ethic. The people-pleaser in her hates turning people away, so her meetings tend to run much longer than scheduled, creating calendar chaos and eating into rare free space to work on important projects. She feels guilty about not exercising and not spending more time with family and friends, but she can't seem to pull away. Until Pam recognizes, names, and tames her accidental identities and consciously chooses another path, she—and the people who matter most to her—will suffer.

Mike is a technology vice president who was known for being tough on people. He was unpredictable—affable one minute, then angry and scolding the next. After watching him lead a meeting, I debriefed with him and dubbed him "mad dad" for the way he spoke to his team when they didn't meet his standards. (Not a very sophisticated analogy, but it landed.) I asked him how he wanted to be known. He responded, "I want to be known as a passionate, caring leader who helps people achieve things they didn't know they could achieve." Yet, his behaviors were aligned with a different subconscious belief—that he (and everyone else in his life) had to be perfect. Mistakes weren't allowed. Given that mistakes are unavoidable, you can imagine how this belief got him into trouble. This unintentional identity, formed by being raised by a perfectionist father and spending twenty years in a command-and-control military environment (where mistakes could be fatal and standards were accordingly very high), thwarted his good intentions because when mistakes happened (as they always do), he'd become fearful. And his fear-based reactions including yelling at subordinates, and keeping what he deemed bad news from leaders while he tried to clean it up.

Recall Tom from Chapter Three, who had an intern mentality, despite his Vice President title? He had a story about being unworthy to walk on the twenty-eighth floor where all the high-paid senior executives sat. In Tom's mind, he was still that intern from more than two decades ago. I asked him to "Imagine you're home and have a broken pipe under your sink that's flooding your kitchen. When the plumber arrives, how do you view him?" He said, "He's my hero coming to the rescue." I asked, "What would you think if that plumber came into your house cowering because your house was so beautiful and he didn't feel worthy?" He said, "I wouldn't have much confidence in him." Tom then realized that he was the hero on the twenty-eighth floor, coming in with knowledge and expertise that only he could provide. This subtle identity shift helped him be his most helpful and intelligent self with whomever he spoke.

My own aspirational identity story sounds something like: *Courageous illuminator, restoring brilliance anywhere with authenticity, wit, compassion, and wisdom.* But, my subconscious identity was all about keeping the peace and following the rules. When I was very young, my mom would introduce me with: "This is Denise. She's shy." I eschewed conflict and rarely spoke up unless it was in the classroom, where I excelled as both student and class jester. I was the perfect student, never allowing myself to miss a deadline or score less than an A. This identity served me in several ways: I won a regent scholarship and eventually earned a master's from Stanford. But it came with a high price: I was filled with anxiety and fear that I would make a misstep; and my conflict avoidance kept me out of arguments, but it also filled me with resentment and anger about unresolved issues.

It's no mystery how I developed this story. Growing up an only child who eventually became the prize in a vicious custody battle, this identity was my means of creating peace and order in what felt like a chaotic world where I had little control. During a very ugly time between my parents, I essentially played possum (my parasympathetic nervous system in freeze mode) to avoid toxic conversations. To this day, I can still be lured by that need to be liked, to avoid conflict, and to crawl into my hermit shell with Netflix and or a good book. It has also led to me avoiding taking risks in business, or asking for support. But look back at my desired identity story: *Courageous illuminator, restoring brilliance anywhere with authenticity, wit, compassion, and wisdom.* There's very little illumination or courage in my accidentally crafted identity, which was all about crawling into a ball. But after years of reminding myself of what I want to create in the world, I have my brilliance back. It's ongoing work. Your protective identity story won't stop talking to you. But you can stop listening, believing, and acting as though it were true. A few years ago, a leader who'd known me for years introduced me to her team before a workshop by saying, "We're in good hands today. This is Denise . . . and she's fearless." Clearly, my efforts to shift my identity story had affected how I was perceived and the difference I could make.

I recently helped a client "upgrade" his identity story that he believes stemmed from something that happened when he was five years old. Jim, who's now in his late forties, told me that when he entered kindergarten, he experienced severe stress and separation anxiety. A less than empathetic teacher told him and his parents that he was incapable of learning and would likely always be held back. Jim and his parents believed him.

As we learned in Chapter Two, a belief's job is to collect supporting evidence and delete or refute contradictory evidence. Because of our negativity bias, your brain is better at finding evidence that supports a negative identity. You have to consciously look for evidence that you are the person you want to be. I asked Jim what evidence he had this belief was true. He said, "Not much, though I often compare myself to others and I don't measure up." Then I asked him what evidence he had that the story was false. He had ample: he graduated with honors, earned a master's degree, excelled at work, was loved by his direct reports, and had never been fired or laid off.

In the beginning, your new identity will feel fraudulent, as it did for Jim who told me, "For an instant, I feel that the new identity is right, but I can't hold on to that feeling." I told him that was normal. For a thought to stick, we have to repeat it until two single neurons blossom into what look like thick bushes (or as scientists like to say, *neurons that fire together wire together*). Jim's been repeating the old thought for decades, so we had to find cues to help him repeat the new thought over and over so he could catch up and supplant the old one. I also gave him the positivity app e-Catch the Feeling to help his brain quickly develop more neurons for positive thinking.

To embed the new identity, you need to reinforce it through *repeated small wins*. So if your new identity is "I'm a runner," rather than set a goal of running five miles on your first day, then beating yourself up because you failed to do it, walk for five minutes. Then consciously celebrate that success. Tomorrow you can do the same. Or walk a little more. Stop and acknowledge the success and how the behavior reinforces your new identity.

Change won't happen overnight, but it *will* happen. Notice incremental improvements instead of anticipating massive change. Get a digital scale and celebrate every ounce lost or every percentage change in body fat. Celebrate that you ran one block farther than you did yesterday, or spent five more minutes with your child instead of your laptop. Let these small wins reinforce your new identity. If you hold to your new identity, you will see inevitable failures as minor, and get back on track. By intentionally choosing actions aligned with your aspirational identity, you'll one day notice that you've become the person you want to be, the person you were meant to be, and who the world needs you to be.

Putting it All Together

For years, I tried to lose the weight I gained while pregnant. It was a big *should* on my list. And I made some progress by following the "slow carb" plan in Tim Ferriss's book,

The 4-Hour Body. But I hit a plateau. I then decided to make this my *must*. I switched my identity from someone who would just have to settle for my post-baby body, to someone who looked and felt younger than her years, and who inspired my daughter in the way I took care of and felt about myself. I felt extreme frustration (pain) with my current state and extreme pleasure envisioning wearing a smaller size and having more energy.

Then I gathered the support and created the structures I needed to become that person hiding inside me. I hired a nutritionist from my doctor's office who put me on a very regimented, customized plan that, while difficult, was so well defined that it was easy to know what was allowed and what was not. I needed that kind of structure without ambiguity. I did it with my then husband, making it a thousand times easier because I was able to remove all forbidden foods from the house. I took these incremental baby steps before ever starting the program. Here's another reason a *must* is more potent than a *should*: one hundred percent commitment is easier than eighty percent.

When you're only eighty percent committed, you have to constantly assess if this will be the time you stray. That takes mental fortitude we can't afford. When you're a hundred percent committed, you find a way.

> *Our doubts are traitors,*
> *And makes us lose the good we oft might win,*
> *By fearing to attempt.*
>
> —William Shakespeare,
> *Measure for Measure*

After hiring the nutritionist and getting the meal plan, I rid my house of my favorite indulgences. I threw out the dark chocolate and gave away the corkscrew. I stuffed my cabinets and fridge with lean meats and vegetables. I created meal plans and ate on a regular schedule. I didn't dine out or eat takeout. It wasn't easy. In fact, it sucked. But I was finally a hundred percent committed and had the right support and structures. I wouldn't have gone to such lengths if I wasn't a hundred percent committed. And the results I saw provided me with so much pleasure that I kept going. After years of trying, I achieved—and surpassed—my goal in three months. That was three years ago. Not only did I not gain the weight back, I lost a few more pounds because of the new habits I created. And I was so pleased with my results and pained by the idea of regression that I'm motivated to keep it up.

I was rewired.

Temptations won't disappear, nor will people trying to pull you to the dark side, but you can plan for them. And when you're one hundred percent committed, you will act in your best interests. I'd love to tell you that your old habits will get replaced, but unfortunately, they linger. While some old habits/cravings may never die, you can absolutely weaken undesirable habits and create stronger ones. If you set yourself up for success with the right environment and support, you can achieve and maintain anything. Too often, I hear that someone broke their good streak and, assuming they were weak, gave up and went back to their old ways. Maybe you've done it yourself: stuck with a diet and then instead of forgiving yourself when you eat that piece of cake, you decide, "Well, I might as well give up on that goal and eat the whole cake." Christine Carter, PhD, calls this the "What the Hell Effect."

When you do give in to instinct—and you will—don't beat yourself up. Know that your brain was trying to protect you. Look at the situation objectively and note what factors contributed to the breakdown. Were you in Starbucks mid-afternoon when your sugar craving was high? Did you forget to eat before you went shopping for groceries? Did you forget to bring your lunch to work? Food journals, diet plans, meal prep, exercise buddies, padlocks on the fridge, and e-mail updates to your coach are all examples of structures that will help support you. Make adjustments, and then get back on your program. Be rational, not emotional.

You'll shock yourself with what you can do. Before I lost the weight, if you'd told me that I'd be able to throw out my Spanx, I would have been very skeptical. But four years later, I'm still on the other side of my goal, stronger and leaner than I've ever been (with the possible exception of high school) all because I made my goal a must, then gathered the right kind of support for my needs. I'm proof that Tim Ferriss' belief that you can revamp your body with minimal time and effort holds true. And my daily two-and-a-half-mile power walk in the hills doesn't even feel like exercise. It feels like an addiction that helps me stay sane, grateful, energized, productive, grounded, creative, and happy.

Let's sum up where we've been …

You're not a bad person if you've failed to stick with a plan, or if you've achieved a goal and then backtracked; you were a victim of your brain's very powerful need to avoid the pain of change and move you toward pleasure.

If you want to achieve a goal, you must work with the fact that your brain doesn't want you to change. You must follow these steps to trick your brain into following your plan until new habits are wired.

As a reminder, if you want to achieve a goal, you must avoid these common self-sabotaging mistakes:

- Making the first step too big and daunting.
- Choosing the wrong goal.
- Relying on willpower and failing to establish support and structures.

To ensure your success, do this instead:

- Choose a focus area that is so painful you can't stand the status quo any longer.
- Create an inspiring vision before choosing a specific target.
- Take an immediate baby step toward that vision today, and start building momentum toward audacious results.
- Set yourself up for success by:
    - Getting adequate support
    - Creating structures, reminders, and rituals
    - Removing temptation
    - Savoring extrinsic and intrinsic rewards
    - Upgrading your old identity

Finally, savor every step of your success and forgive your inevitable setbacks. Few of us take time to really appreciate our incremental, and, eventually, monumental achievements.

Go ahead now and start turning your *must do* into a very gratifying *I did*. Your better self is waiting.

Until one is committed, there is hesitancy,
the chance to draw back, always ineffectiveness.
Concerning all acts of initiative (and creation),
there is one elementary truth, the ignorance
of which kills countless ideas and splendid plans:
that the moment one definitely commits oneself,
then Providence moves too. All sorts of things occur
to help one that would never otherwise have occurred.
A whole stream of events issues from the decision,
raising in one's favor all manner of unforeseen incidents
and meetings and material assistance, which
no man could have dreamt would have come his way.
Whatever you can do, or dream you can, begin it.
Boldness has genius, power, and magic in it!
Begin it now.

—W.H. MURRAY

REFLECTION QUESTIONS

1. What's your current cue for the habit you want to quit or change? (For me, cooking dinner was my unintentional cue to pour a glass of wine.)

2. What will be your intentional cue(s) to do the new behavior?

3. Take a look at the inspiring vision you created earlier. Who would you need to be in order to achieve that?

CHAPTER TEN:

How to Say No
with Grace, Not Guilt

*The difference between successful people
and really successful people is that
really successful people say no
to almost everything.*
—WARREN BUFFETT

I have a fundamental belief that we have *infinite potential and limited capacity.* We are all constrained by time: twenty-four hours in a day—eight of which are needed for sleep—and a limited and unknown number of days to live. And we're all constrained by bodies that need constant fuel, rest, and renewal. When we defy these realities and extend beyond our body's capacity, we break in myriad ways (obesity, autoimmune disorders, illness, and injuries). So, if our vulnerability is so obvious yet our capacity for achievement so great, why do we live our lives as though the inverse were true: that we have *infinite capacity and limited potential?* Why, in other words, do we live small, stressed-out existences that too often end in regret? Again, we can trace it to our brain's need to keep us safe.

When we ignore our limitations and say yes too often, we can experience exhaustion, distraction, quality slippage, and more. We also experience emotional pain in the form of *guilt and resentment*. Guilt arises when we feel like we're letting people down by giving too little. Like all emotions, guilt serves as a messenger; its purpose is to signal that we've done something wrong and need to make amends. But most of us have oversensitive guilt triggers. The only good news about guilt is that if you're feeling it often, there's a good chance you aren't a sociopath. Congratulations.

At the other end of the emotional spectrum is resentment, the emotion we feel when we believe we've given more than our fair share (and others need to pull their own damn weight). Resentment's purpose is to signal that we've overextended ourselves and have probably said yes too often, and/or failed to ask for the support we need. When we hold on to resentment, it wears on our health and happiness.

Resentment is like drinking poison and then hoping it will kill your enemies.

—NELSON MANDELA

Not only does resentment dampen our mood, it eats away at us from the inside and harms our relationships. How do you act toward others when you're feeling resentful? Perhaps you make snarky comments, avoid people, roll your eyes, or fail to acknowledge and show appreciation. No matter how you express it, your target can probably feel the resentment oozing out of you, and no one likes to be on the receiving end of resentment.

One single word tells you that you're letting guilt or resentment drive your decisions. That word is *should*. When we feel guilt, we tell ourselves "I should . . . leave work earlier / listen to my kids without checking my phone / exercise more / eat healthier," and so on. When we feel resentment, we tell ourselves "He/She/They should . . . do more around the house / give me a raise / thank me more often / eat their vegetables."

As we saw in Chapter Eight where you listed all the things you regularly tell yourself you should do, *shoulds* don't motivate us: they just make us feel awful. Yet, we'd rather feel these emotions and experience the consequences than design days that align with our goals and values. We'd rather say yes habitually than experience the pain of designing a day where we have to decline requests and ask for support.

Corporate Culture and Saying No

Fortunately, it's becoming abundantly clear in many companies that people need to work smarter and live better. Look at the top business titles and you'll see that life and work are becoming more integrated, with an emphasis on self-care. We see companies teaching mindfulness, creating quiet rooms, and conducting meetings outside.

I recently gave my "Say No with Grace, Not Guilt" talk at Kaiser Permanente, a sixty-billion-dollar health insurance and care provider. I was told that the room would hold forty people. Instead, we had fifty people in the room and more than four hundred participating via live video stream. Turns out, several executives in the company enthusiastically encouraged their employees to attend. One senior vice president canceled his staff meeting and encouraged all his executive direct reports to attend with their teams.

Perhaps you're thinking "This will never fly at my company: *yes* might as well be our motto and *no* is the fastest way to get shown the door." I readily admit that few startups hire me to do this talk. Many tech startups hire young talent and work people to the bone. Still, few leaders want their people working on low priority tasks. They want you to be effective and use your time wisely. And no boss wants you to end up on medical leave.

In this chapter, I'll teach you both overt and subtle ways to decline requests so that you are viewed as a high performer with a backbone, who others *should* emulate, regardless of your company culture. Before we get to the three brain-based nuisances that keep us overburdened, I'd like revisit my client, Ellen, who we met in Chapter One.

I was sitting at a small round table in a corner office on the twenty-second floor with Ellen, a director at a multibillion-dollar health company, and her boss, a highly respected senior vice president, who's known for having high expectations of herself and others. Not only does she rarely hear the word no, she's accustomed to people acting swiftly at nearly any request. She hired me to help support Ellen, and this was my chance to share the stakeholder feedback and coaching program plan with both of them.

I told them that I'd rarely heard such high praise as I did from Ellen's employees and clients: people universally respected and appreciated her. They also cared. In fact, several expressed concern that she'd taken too much on—

that her scope of work was enough to keep several people busy. A few people even told me they were worried about her health and how much longer she could keep up her pace. I suspect they also worried about how on earth all the work would get done, and get done well, if Ellen were to break.

Then I presented what I expected would be the most controversial aspect of the plan. I told the boss (who was paying my fees) that her very smart, talented, reliable director needed to learn to prioritize and say no, or that the boss would end up looking for her in the hospital. I also told her that I thought it would be the most difficult behavior for Ellen to change. I asked the boss if she could support Ellen in saying no.

The boss paused for a moment, took a breath, and said, "This is absolutely right. You have my full backing that this is the right goal. That said, don't expect me to be a good role model, or to even make this easy. It's up to you to prioritize and decide what you can and cannot do. It's going to be up to you to work with Denise on this. I promise to try to respect it." I appreciated the vice president's honesty. If you're waiting for your boss to notice you're overextended, you might wait a very long time.

Your boss expects you to be a grown-up who can weigh tasks against all that you know about the department goals, and prioritize accordingly. It's up to you to deliver what may feel like bad news at times, and to ask for additional support as needed. Sure, some people are lazy and have to be prodded to take on work. But most of my clients are like Ellen: intelligent, hard-working, committed people who don't want to let down their clients, bosses, business partners, or teams. And to them, declining requests feels like they're doing just that.

As a result, we have an epidemic of overstretched, burned-out people-pleasers who are wasting their energy and brilliance on the wrong things.

The Three Pains in the Brain

Why do so many people say yes to things they don't have time, energy, or passion for? It boils down to two basic human needs that we talked about earlier in the book: the need to avoid pain and the need to feel pleasure. We also all have a deep need to feel connected to others. One of the ways we satisfy this need is to help others, and to, thereby, feel needed and appreciated. But when we help others beyond our capacity, the reward of appreciation is accompanied, or even replaced by, our own feelings of resentment and regret. Thus, our attempt to create pleasure ends up resulting mostly in pain. And as I mentioned earlier, avoiding pain is the bigger motivator. When you consider that there are at least three giant pains at play when we even consider saying no, it's no wonder that we say yes beyond our capacity, and yes to things that aren't aligned with our highest intentions, values, and goals.

PAIN #1: SOCIAL PAIN

In Chapter Four, we learned how social pain is perhaps the worst of all emotional and physical pains. Social pain prompts us to say yes in order to avoid exclusion and resentment. We're willing to sacrifice our own needs and desires to avoid the feeling of disconnection. While men and women both experience social pain, women probably have it worse. Until recently, women did not have legal rights or authority (and sadly, this is still the case in many parts of the world). Rather, women were valued for their role as nurturers, not on the merit of their ideas and efforts. Thus, women had to learn to survive through their ability to connect and influence without official authority. Women needed to be liked, or they would live lives as "old maids" (or burned as witches).

PAIN #2: STATUS PAIN

Status pain stems from comparison and telling ourselves that *we aren't as good as others.* This story accompanies an emotion that's even stronger and more toxic than guilt: shame. As Brené Brown explains in her book *Daring Greatly,* guilt is the feeling that we've *done* something bad; shame is the feeling that we *are* bad. Brown's research showed that men and women feel shame for different reasons. At the top of the list for women are motherhood (or nurturer) and appearance. For men, it's about success and being an effective breadwinner. In cultures where both men and women work and care for children, there's probably more overlap.

> *We have a deep-seated conviction that more work, more enrichment activities for the kids, more likes on Facebook or Instagram, more stuff would be better. Unless we like feeling exhausted and overwhelmed, we need to accept that more is not necessarily better . . .*
>
> —CHRISTINE CARTER, PhD

How did we develop this status pain? It may have something to do with our early development. Humans are born completely helpless and dependent, and remain so for many years unlike many other species. Zebras start walking moments after being birthed. Tigers move out of the house after a short boot camp with their mom. Neither tigers nor zebras look at one another and ask, "Do these stripes make my butt look big?" Humans, on the other hand, take a big hit to their confidence and innocence when they discover that, without the right cry or giggle, they won't get fed, held, or changed. Over time, we develop feelings of fear and unworthiness. Subconsciously (or overtly), we worry that we aren't good enough. We forget that we are unique and perfect in our own way, deserving of a brilliant life simply because we exist.

Our subtle (or loud) "I'm not good enough" story is a major contributor to feelings of being overwhelmed: we overcommit to prove that we're worthy. We may stay late in the office because we don't want to be the first to leave. We answer the boss's e-mail on Saturday, even though she told us to ignore her e-mails on the weekend. We fail to take vacation and sick days because we don't want to appear lazy or fall behind. We take on projects that we aren't passionate about because we want to get ahead. We strive for promotion even though we may not want the headache that comes with more responsibility. We acquire trappings of success, yet we feel empty and unfulfilled.

PAIN #3: PRIORITIZATION

The third brain-based pain has to do with our finite energy reserves. Recall from Chapter Five that prioritizing our day is one of the most energy-consuming tasks we can perform. There are so many things to consider—so many perceived threats involved as we think about what we have to say no to—that we often simply don't choose how to spend our time: we let life happen to us instead. We make to-do lists (essentially, "yes-lists") and don't explicitly decide what we'll say no to. Instead we end up accidentally saying no to tasks vital to our brilliance.

How to Say No with Grace in Six Steps

Declining requests is easier once you have the right language. According to author and psychotherapist Anne Brown, most of us avoid the word no because we don't want to hear it said to us. We want to save others and ourselves from feeling rejected. Here's some good news: You can decline requests without actually saying no. Here's how to do it effectively, so the message is clear, and your reputation enhanced.

1. CREATE A PAUSE

It's much easier to decline first than it is to undo a yes. You need to buy yourself time before you inadvertently say yes, because you only have roughly three hundredths of a second before your mouth blurts. The same goes for e-mail, as too many of us have learned the hard way. (Damn you, "Reply All!") Before you respond to a request, take a deep breath. This will give you time to craft a verbal or written response that doesn't feel quite natural yet. If you're not sure what to say, you can buy time with language like "Let me check my calendar and get back to you by the end of the day" or, "Let me give this some thought: I don't want to commit only to tell you later that I can't do it after all." Be sure to follow up as promised, or you risk harming your credibility.

2. CLEARLY DECLINE

Here are a few options that will be easier to deliver and swallow than a pure no:

- "I can't."
- "I'm not available."
- "I'm not able."
- "I wish I could but I'm already committed."
- "I would love to be able to do that for you but I just can't."
- "Not today."
- "No, thank you."

Notice the clarity? There are no "mights," no "tries." Don't worry if these sound terse. This is only the first step. We'll add more language in a bit.

3. SHARE A CREDIBLE REASON

You might find it easier and more effective to share a reason. You're likely to have a number of reasons to decline. Some may include: you don't have time; you'll be out of town; you'd rather do taxes than any favor for this person; and the last time you watched their dog, he peed on your new couch. While these may be true, they won't help you improve your relationships and reputation. Share an honest explanation that you think is most credible *to them*.

For example, if you can't make a meeting because you have to take your sick dog to the vet, choose how much detail you share depending on whether the recipient is a dog lover. If they aren't, or you don't know, you could simply say, "I have a personal commitment," or "I have to go to the doctor." Both are true, but less specific.

When I was working at Charles Schwab, I was lucky enough to work in a culture that emphasized the importance of work–life balance for all employees. One of our senior executives had even authored a popular book on the topic. This made it easy for me to optimistically share the company values with a huge room of new hires every Monday morning. I was fond of telling people, "We don't care if you have to walk your bird every day at 5:30 PM; that's your business." One day someone came to me after the session and said, "I can't believe you said that. I have a thirty-year-old parrot who is family to me and we go on walks each evening."

Who am I to judge?

Here are some examples of what it might sound like to decline at work:

I'd like to but I'm unable to because . . .

- my team is down two people and we're already working nights and weekends.

- I have another commitment at the same time that I can't move.
- I'll be on vacation (on Mars).
- this isn't my area of expertise and I'm afraid that I'd deliver you a subpar product.
- we'd have to drop the high priority project we're working on.

Recently, I was giving this talk to a large audience. After having them read their decline to a neighbor and get feedback, I asked how it went and what they had learned. One woman said she learned that she needed to share more context about *why* she couldn't take on the request. I asked her to tell me what she had told her partner. She said, "I can't take that on because I'm immersed in a big project right now and have a firm deadline." She said her partner wanted to know what the "big project" was. I asked her to reframe what she thought the lesson of that exchange was and offered this alternative: that her partner in this exercise needs more context, but for many people, what she shared would suffice. Many heads nodded in agreement.

The more you know about a person, the better you can tailor your message. Some people—particularly fast-paced, driver types—will appreciate your brevity and clarity and will move on to figuring out how to get the job done without you. More creative or sensitive types may want more information. Err on the side of clarity and brevity, and have more explanation on hand should you need it. If you don't have a reason that you believe they'd respect, don't offer one. Or give a general reason. You can say simply: "Thank you for asking. I wish I could but I have another obligation." And if they push you, you can say, "My reason is personal."

4. OFFER SINCERE GRATITUDE (AS RELEVANT)

If you can't find anything to be grateful for, leave this step out, but I'm guessing that you can find something that you're sincerely grateful for. It may sound like: "Thank you for trusting me with this," or "Thank you for considering me." Some people suggest you put the "thank you" first. I like putting it after the decline because research shows that people pay more attention to endings than beginnings. So, ending with gratitude can soften a decline. If it feels more natural, you can move the thank-you to the beginning.

5. MAKE AN OFFER

Only make an offer if you have one and if it *serves both people's needs*. Do not make an offer simply to make yourself feel better. Do that, and you're likely to end up overcommitting. One client shared a great strategy. When her company bought a new scanner, she took it upon herself to learn how to use it. People started asking her to scan their documents for them. Before too long, she had piles on her desk from nearly everyone on the floor. Resentment was building in her because she was taking time from her already packed day to do something others were capable of doing. Smartly, she came up with a strategy before she acted out of resentment. She told people that she was no longer able to scan their documents and that she would like to conduct two training sessions that week to demonstrate and answer questions. With that offer, she freed herself up and empowered others at the same time. Everyone won.

Another client was asked to serve as president on a prestigious industry board. He really wanted to say yes, as he believed that the role would help his professional reputation. However, it would also make it harder for him to finish his PhD—his clear priority. He declined, sharing with them that while he'd like to do it, it would distract him from finishing his dissertation (a reason that the asker considered credible). He then offered to take the position the following year. Your offer could sound like: "I know of a good resource, would you like her information?" or "Would you like me to ask a few people if they're available?"

6. DROP THE GUILT

Recall that guilt only serves us when it indicates an area where we've acted outside the boundaries of our integrity. Beyond that, guilt can trick us into thinking we're actually doing something productive: for example, "At least *I* feel guilty about not donating to that charity. *You*, on the other hand, are just fine with your selfishness."

When you feel guilt, ask yourself, "Have I harmed someone or acted in conflict with my values?" If yes, apologize, then do better. Most times, guilt is just a bad habit—the result of trying to live up to unrealistic, unattainable standards.

APPLYING THIS IN THE WORKPLACE

Obviously, work is different from personal life. In business, you have a contractual obligation to fulfill your duties. That said, you still have constraints of time and energy. Your job isn't to say yes; it's to be effective. Just as companies have to make choices about how to invest money, individuals have to decide how to invest their intellect and energies. Say yes to the wrong things and you risk diminishing your impact. My clients don't come to me saying that they have trouble saying no. Instead, they talk about "time management," "productivity," or "work–life balance." Once we take a look at how they spend their precious time and how they respond to requests at work and in their personal lives, they realize there is no way in hell they can do everything on their list (let alone do it well), and that many things on their list aren't even worth their attention. When they get clear on their priorities, they panic a bit with the realization that they're going to have to begin declining requests and saying no to certain habits.

You can't expect someone else to set boundaries for you. It's rare that a boss will preface a request with "I really want you to say no if you don't have time or a desire to do this." (As a manager, I did this, but given my acute awareness of limitations, I'm not normal!) I learned this the hard way. Upon starting a new job, I reinjured a ruptured disk in my spine. I kept telling myself that it would be fine, that I needed to keep working (to prove myself worthy). Going on leave six months into the job felt like a non-option. After about two weeks, I could no longer sit, so I attended meetings standing up. After another couple of weeks, I had to attend longer meetings lying down on my back (really). Finally, when I could no longer take a step without agony, I found myself on an operating table, then off work for four weeks. Later, the head of my department asked, "Why didn't you take care of that sooner, before it got so bad? I wish you would have said something."

If you manage people, I strongly encourage you to have a "say no" meeting with your team. The lower you are in an organization, the harder it is to summon the courage to decline requests. Take initiative to facilitate a team discussion where you identify work that is low value or that could be done more efficiently. My 4-D Conversation—(Drop, Delegate, Do, and Do Differently from Chapter Five) can guide you. You can also grab a template from www.brillianceinc.com/resources.

THE GIFT OF AN EARLY, EXPLICIT NO

Many people think that declining requests means that we won't be available to others or that we're selfish. In fact, the opposite is true. Saying yes when you don't have the capacity is no gift. Have you ever had someone say yes to you, then deliver unreliable service? Perhaps they took too long to deliver. Or maybe they did the job poorly. Or perhaps they complained about it, or just plain old failed to show up. Wouldn't you rather they'd just told you no in the first place?

> *A "No" uttered from the deepest conviction is better than a "Yes" merely uttered to please, or worse, to avoid trouble.*
>
> —MAHATMA GANDHI

When you tell someone that you're not available, you free them up to find someone else who can do the job better. When you overextend yourself, you're not only less available to others, you don't even have capacity for yourself.

Airlines instruct parents to put their oxygen masks on first for a reason: if you don't have enough capacity, you're less able to serve others and everyone suffers. When you take better care of yourself, you're better able to bring your full energy and talents to others.

Why Change Now?

You didn't just wake up today and decide that you were overcommitted. I'm guessing that you've known for a while that something needed to change. So, before you spend any precious time reading more, ask yourself, "Why change now?" Imagine for a moment that you don't change: that you keep saying yes to others' requests just as you've done up to this point. Then consider: What will your life be like (emotional state, health, relationships, credibility) in six months if you don't take more time for yourself and your priorities? What about in a year?

Look back at your Brilliant Life Assessment results. What did you say was the most important gap? Which item did you decide to upgrade to a *must do*? Now, take a few moments to brainstorm some things you'll say yes and no to, in order to close the gap and increase your satisfaction in that area.

Here's an example using the goal of spending more quality time with family:

YES:	NO:
Planning meals in advance and keeping kitchen stocked	Checking e-mail or texts after the table is set for dinner
Using Instacart or another grocery delivery service so we have more time together on the weekends	Bringing laptop home
Coming up with great conversation starters at dinner	Checking e-mail on weekends after the family is awake

In the moment you say yes to one thing, *you're saying no to every other possibility.* You have the same number of hours in a day as everyone else. Your values, on the other hand, are specific to you. How you spend your resources should reflect those values.

Nature respects the laws of finite capacity, and never struggles with the choice. If you observe a climbing star jasmine vine, the tendrils neglect to grow leaves or fragrant flowers until the plant has capacity. It knows the tradeoff: remain a bush and sprout lots of leaves and flowers, or climb and postpone the abundance. Even more inspiring to me is the magnolia tree. The magnolia produces what, in my mind, is the most magnificent display of flowers nature offers. Yet, if you look closely, the magnolia sacrifices leaves once they've done their work providing the required nutrients—a necessary action with brilliant results; the magnolia never laments the loss.

If we recognized our potential, were clear about our priorities, and were honest about our limitations, our choices would be as clear—and brilliant—as the magnolia.

Make it Real: Plan for Your Difficult Case

With whom do you find it most difficult to say no? Your boss? A friend? A certain relative? For me, I used to feel the most anxiety and guilt walking by clipboard-toting volunteers standing outside my local market. The really good ones had a great one-liner like, "Do you have thirty seconds to help homeless kids?" Now, what schlep would say no to that? Surely only the most selfish, evil person. Then I discovered my cure and I set clear, guilt-free boundaries. Here's my process. First, I deliberately choose a few charities that have deep meaning for me and I give to them. I set up an auto-contribute system and I'm done. Back on the street, I acknowledge the volunteer by smiling and making eye contact. Can you imagine how many people don't even acknowledge them? How exhausting it must be to feel invisible? Then I decline by simply saying, "Not today." Then I add, with deep sincerity and without guilt, "Thank you for doing this important work." Sometimes I even add a reason: "I already gave." They don't need to know that I gave to a different charity.

Declining requests and asking for support is about much more than time management. It's about life management: potential management. People need you—

not to say yes to everything thrown at you—but to be your most brilliant version of you. I know you can do this. Please, for the sake of all, say *yes* to your brilliance. You now have the steps and scripts. I suggest, as I tell all my workshop participants, that you try it *before* you feel ready, because if you wait until you have no fear of saying no, nothing will change.

> *You can choose courage*
> *or you can choose comfort.*
> *You cannot have both.*
>
> —BRENÉ BROWN

REFLECTION QUESTIONS

1. Select a task you find challenging to decline.

   - What will you say to decline?

   - What reason will you give that is most credible to the other party?

   - What will you offer that will benefit both parties?

   - How will you express gratitude?

2. To whom can you read this decline for practice and to get feedback about your clarity, tone, and overall effectiveness? (Aim for someone who knows the target recipient.)

Conclusion

I said early on in the book that this wasn't about finding "balance." I think that word is not just overused, but misleading—as if your life will magically become fulfilled (and your potential unleashed) if you spend more time at home, and less at work. I suggested we aim instead for integration—between our inner world of thoughts, emotions, and health, and our outer world of relationships, behaviors, and physical surroundings. Yesterday, I had a get-to-know-you conversation with a new client who wanted to work on work–life balance. When I asked her what she meant by "balance" she said it was "complicated." She went on to tell me about how she had taken a demotion after becoming completely burned out in a toxic work environment. She said that her new job was great, and that her family life had improved tremendously, but that she had extreme guilt about not working very hard, and also felt a sense of loss of purpose now that she didn't manage a huge organization. She quoted Brené Brown: "The antidote to exhaustion isn't rest. It's wholeheartedness." I knew then that we were going to have a great time, and that she was going to make great progress. I told her about my Brilliant Life Assessment and she said bring it on. I also told her that she needed to give herself a break, because to her brain, she might as well have been in a war zone while she was working for two years under the reign of a toxic leader.

This book has also *not* been about finding happiness. I've nothing against happiness. What bugs me is that our culture's obsession with happiness actually causes us great distress. What happens when we feel sadness, anger, resentment, or other important emotions? We may feel guilt or shame for our lack of happiness, and we may even tamp other instructive emotions down, failing to listen to them and honor them. I'm all for amplifying emotions like love, gratitude, peace, compassion, and forgiveness. Like happiness, all these emotions fill us with neurotransmitters that help us feel good and act in ways that help us be more creative, connected, and content. I'm also in favor of finding emotional flow (instead of stagnation or habit), where our emotions arise and instruct us so we can consciously decide what best action to take. When emotions like anger cease to be just instructive, but grow into toxic habitual reactions, we must learn to tame them.

My first working title for this book was *Path to Brilliance*. Through input from my tribe, I came to realize it was uninspiring, intimidating, and misleading. I'd love to write the book that contains the magical *Six Steps to the Life of Your Dreams!* but that book would be a lie. If I were forced to describe achieving work–life brilliance in a few steps, those steps would include:

1. Assess
2. Choose
3. Change

Assess

Assess your life from the inside out: brain, body, behaviors, relationship, and environment. Then ask yourself, where are you aligned and where are you out of whack? This is no easy task. It takes vulnerability, honesty, and courage. It's tempting to compare ourselves to others and/or to some ideal vision we have for ourselves. It took me a long time before I could honestly assess my life without comparing it to some ideal that I crafted—not from my heart's desire, but from comparison. I anxiously sought to be the "best" daughter and student I could be, make the "best" decisions about jobs, marry a life partner in my twenties, travel the world, and live in a beautiful house in a stunning, idyllic neighborhood. It's not that any of these are bad things: it's the way I pursued them that was misguided. I filled my body with toxic stress and failed to listen honestly to my head, heart, and gut. I committed to a relationship, ignoring early warning signs that we weren't ideally matched; I spent beyond my ability to pay for my life; and I struggled with existential angst about finding my calling. So. Much. Struggling. So little ease and just enjoying, observing, and learning from the moments. And, as Victoria Castle writes, "If struggling were the way to get there, we'd all be there by now."

I'll never forget my first appointment with Dr. Raj Patel. I was broken by my car accident, rheumatoid arthritis, and stress about what my life would look like in the future. I'd just humiliated myself in an interview for Stanford's PhD program. (I wasn't yet clear that academia was a horrible fit for me, and I was just seeking the familiarity in the cocoon I'd excelled in.) I told Dr. Patel that I feared

I'd make a misstep and throw my life into chaos, such that I'd never reach my potential. He paused and said, "What happens if Denise makes a mistake?" I don't know if it was the way he phrased it in the third person or just that my subconscious needed to hear it, but that question released something inside me, and tears started uncontrollably pouring down my face. He calmly handed me a tissue box as if this happened all the time. I felt a huge sense of relief and laughed (as I cried) about the absurdity of my quest for perfection. What would happen if I made a "mistake?" The world would continue to turn . . . and I might actually learn something, that's what.

I spoke to my dad this morning and he was looking forward to getting a "fitness assessment" this afternoon, to learn more about what his post hip surgery and shoulder limitations were, so he could work out again without hurting himself. He chuckled that it would be great to get back into shape and catch up with my stepmom, Nancy. Then he said, "I'll never catch up with Nancy." I replied, "Dad, neither will I . . . and that's OK." You see, my stepmom does CrossFit several times a week and is impressively strong and fit. She's never had a broken bone, surgery, or disease, and she abhors going to the doctor and taking medicine. So, when a bone density test showed signs of osteoarthritis she decided to visit her local CrossFit class, rather than the traditional drug treatment. Three years later, a new test shows she's gained bone density. She can also lift her own weight in a squat press. I told my dad, "That's just not who we are." We all just have to make the most of what we've got. If my dad or I tried to keep up with Nance, we'd end up in the hospital. Assess your current state with love and openness instead of guilt, shame, disappointment, and comparison. Accept what is.

Choose

Once you're clear about your current state, choose to focus on the area that's causing you the most pain, and that you're ready to take on. Once you choose, follow the six steps (and avoid the common pitfalls) outlined in this book to change your brain so you can build habits that bring you closer to your ideal life.

Start where you are.

—PEMA CHODRON

I got a lovely e-mail from a former boss today, wishing me well and updating me on her life. She's always been someone with amazing stamina and an overbooked calendar. She told me that she ignored foot pain for a year, ending up with plantar fasciitis on both feet—her right foot broken in two places. She's now vowing to pay more attention to the universe (and her body) telling her she needs to slow down. It won't be easy: living fast and busy is a habit for her. She's been living a few steps out of her body for decades. But it's where she needs to focus, or the universe will continue to send her painful reminders that sideline her.

Recently, I attended a conference with the Academy of Brain-based Leadership. During a panel conversation, the chief science officer was asked what developments he predicted in ten years. He responded that soon, we'll all be wearing monitoring devices that make the Fitbit look primitive—devices that track our blood glucose, vitals, and much more. My imagination conjured up images of a mood ring on steroids, where we'd see our neurotransmitter and hormone levels in a given moment. The data would tell us about our levels of cortisol, testosterone, dopamine, serotonin, oxytocin, etc., before and after conversations.

An app might automatically pop up to help me calm my sympathetic nervous system and boost my vagus nerve, so I can be my most confident, calm self. It would tell us not just how long and deeply we slept, but what imbalances could be inhibiting good sleep. Until then, it's upon us to proactively seek answers about our health so we avoid a sudden scare.

You may decide that an area of life is causing you great pain, but you're not ready to take it on. That's okay. In order to upgrade a *should* to a *must,* you have to be ready to take it on wholeheartedly. My ex-husband and I tried to ignore the fact that our marriage was dead in every sense but legal for years. Both of us were allergic to (and I was terrified of) the idea of divorce. I remember listening to Tony Robbins's audio program daily, skipping over the relationship portion because I was afraid of what I would hear. I wasn't ready to pull my head out of the sand and take an honest appraisal. Both our parents had put us through difficult divorces and we didn't want to do the same to our daughter. It was also a logistical nightmare, as those of you who've been through it know. So, until the pain of staying together became bigger than the pain of divorce, we avoided the decision.

The big exception to this avoidance rule is your health. Until we get the futuristic Fitbit, you have to summon the courage and make the time to assess and heal your body, or risk facing a calamitous detour from achieving your potential.

Change

This week, while on my way to a parent-teacher conference, I stopped to marvel at a third-grade project depicting a brain. Each child had colored in one side of the brain with vibrant colors, leaving the other side in dull black and white. On the black and white side, they wrote three debilitating thoughts like: "I'm terrible at math"; "Mistakes are bad"; and "I'm not popular." Then, on the colorful side, they wrote upgraded thoughts like: "Mistakes help me learn faster"; "I make friends when I'm kind and myself"; and "Working through math problems grows my brain." Can you imagine how life could be different if we learn this upgrade skill at a young age?

You are your only border. Throw yourself over it.

—Attributed to Hafiz (in Nielsen's *A Night Divided*)

Lighten Up

We've covered some heavy topics together. And now I make this request: please hold this all lightly. Bring a sense of wonder, gratitude, and humor to this quest to honestly assess and selectively improve yourself. When I broke down in Dr. Patel's office, I was giggling as much as I was crying. I was laughing at the absurdity of my quest for perfection, and crying at the relief I was experiencing as a result of someone asking me a question and then giving me the space and time to have any reaction.

Listen to Brené Brown to hear how someone who researches shame and vulnerability speaks about it with lightness (and lots of swearing). Read Hafiz, who wrote about the mysteries of God and the universe with comedic reverence. Watch Tony Robbins in the documentary *I Am Not Your Guru* to see how someone uses foul language and humor to trick the brain into new patterns. And watch stupid cat videos, read smut, and do whatever else keeps you from taking life so seriously that you forget to feel joy. I will never forget an unusual piece of advice that came from my brilliant mentor James Flaherty. When I asked a question about working deeply with a client he said, "Denise, watch more TV." His point was that almost no client would be ready to work at the level I was asking about, and that I'd become out of touch and unrelatable if I didn't also immerse myself in some pop culture. On a similar note, one day I asked my high school friend Kristy, who works for the United Nations, how on earth she could come back from her missions and listen to people's idle complaints. She said that she always made sure to stream popular American TV shows so she never lost touch with our world, and would have something in common with us lesser angels.

It seems fitting that I'm writing this chapter on my forty-sixth birthday, the day I get to reflect upon and celebrate life. It also seems fitting that my birthday is on the soulful Día de los Muertos (Day of the Dead). None of us knows how many days on earth we have left. My brilliantly illuminated friend Christy, who I met in 1999 at a coaching course at New Ventures West, had only thirty-three birthdays before she was taken suddenly, one month before her daughter's first birthday. In Christy's case, she was a rare light that found its brilliance early and touched many lives. When I last spoke with her, she was working with the very real exhaustion of being a new mom and the stress that can come between parents trying to figure out how to share care and be kind to one another when their brains are fried from sleep deprivation. She had to take a break from healing the world and focus on her immediate physical and relationship needs.

Just as there is no one clear path, there is no destination called Brilliance, where we can set up camp and retire with drink in hand; there are only moments. We are a messy, beautiful, constantly changing work in progress. No matter how evolved you become, life will throw you off. We will all lose our cool. We will all experience stress. We will all get sick. We will all experience profound loss. And (spoiler alert!), we will all die. When we are most brilliant, we can handle life with more ease and grace: we are more resilient, can see more options, and can accept what is. When asked how he never seems to get off balance, the great teacher and founder of Aikido, O Sensei, replied, "I get off balance constantly. I just return so quickly to center you don't notice." That's our goal.

I believe that the greatest of all endeavors is to embrace our beautiful, messy, humanness with honesty, deep compassion, and lightness, and then endeavor to reignite our most brilliant nature.

Live. Now. Brilliantly.

With love and light,

Denise

First, I was dying to finish high school and start college.
And then I was dying to finish college and start working.
Then I was dying to marry and have children.
And then I was dying for my children to grow
old enough so I could go back to work.
And then I was dying to retire.
And now I'm dying . . .
And suddenly I realized I forgot to live.

—UNKNOWN

Recommended Reading

WORKS TO HELP YOU BE YOUR BEST SELF

- *Awaken the Giant Within*, Tony Robbins
- *Brain Rules*, John Medina
- *Born Standing Up: A Comic's Life*, Steve Martin
- *Buddha's Brain*, Rick Hanson, PhD,
  with Richard Mendius, MD
- *Choose Yourself*, James Altucher
- *Daring Greatly*, Brené Brown, PhD
- *Escape from Cubicle Nation*, Pamela Slim
- *Fierce Conversations*, Susan Scott
- *Finding Your Own North Star*, Martha Beck
- *Get Off Your "But,"* Sean Stephenson
- *Getting Things Done*, David Allen
- *Playing Big*, Tara Mohr
- *Power vs. Force*, David R. Hawkins, MD, PhD
- *Success Under Stress*, Sharon Melnick, PhD
- *The Charge*, Brendon Burchard
- *The 4-Hour Body*, Timothy Ferriss
- *The 4-Hour Workweek*, Timothy Ferriss

- *The Power of Habit*, Charles Duhigg
- *The Sleep Revolution*, Arianna Huffington
- *The Spontaneous Fulfillment of Desire*, Deepak Chopra
- *The Success Principles™*, Jack Canfield
- *The Sweet Spot*, Christine Carter, PhD
- *The Trance of Scarcity*, Victoria Castle
- *The Way We're Working Isn't Working*, Tony Schwartz with Jean Gomes and Catherine McCarthy, PhD
- *Tools of Titans*, Tim Ferriss
- *Two Awesome Hours*, Josh Davis, PhD
- *What Got You Here, Won't Get You There*, Marshall Goldsmith with Mark Reiter
- *Wired to Connect*, Amy Banks, MD, with Leigh Ann Hirschman
- *Your Brain at Work*, David Rock

WORKS TO EXPAND AND ENTERTAIN YOUR MIND

- *Art & Physics*, Leonard Shlain
- *Big Magic*, Elizabeth Gilbert
- *Pure Drivel*, Steve Martin
- *The Tao of Physics*, Fritjof Capra

Want More Brilliant Suggestions?
Check out this amazing post by prolific writer, reader, and habit-change expert James Clear, where he organizes hundreds of books by topic:
http://jamesclear.com/best-books

Acknowledgments

I thank my clients for their trust, faith, and courage. I may learn as much from them as they do from me. I want to give a special call-out to Michael Kluzcko and Yesenia Hernandez. Yesenia introduced me to Michael, a senior leader of supply-side operations for a global wine company, back in 2008, when I was struggling with sleep deprivation and its side effects. Michael took a chance on me, hiring me as a trusted advisor for him and his team when I was just starting out on my own. Thanks also to Mike Cerio, an early adopter of my stress workshop. As a coaching client, Mike was always focused on how he could better himself for the sake of his people. When he read my post about stress and saying no with grace, not guilt, he picked up the phone and said, "I need your help." Thanks to a recent merger, workloads were becoming unbearable for his people, and he worried about their health and well-being. Instead of bringing me in for a keynote, we spent two days over two weeks making sure that the ideas and tools were applied so that hundreds of employees could relieve stress and improve their health, relationships, and performance.

I also want to thank the few terrible, toxic leaders I observed during my days in corporate. You helped pique my curiosity about what makes a leader great, and how devastating poor leadership can truly be. I hope, for your sake and those around you, that you found a way to brilliance.

I am so grateful for the amazing people at Kaiser Permanente, where I am both a trusted advisor and a member. They model brilliance, striving every day to make the world a better place though integrated, quality, affordable healthcare. And their leadership, particularly CEO Bernard Tyson, makes my job easier, thanks to his values and how he models the behaviors I'm helping instill in my clients.

I am grateful for this bubble I live in called Oakland, California. Where my daughter knows only diversity, and has friends of every color, religion, and socio-economic status. Where I am seven minutes from hiking trails in the Redwood Regional Park. Where people are flocking because of the weather, culture, people, food, and beauty. Where, in a recent ballot initiative, voters overwhelmingly approved taxes on the most wealthy, rent protections, low-income housing, increased teacher pay, reasonable ammunition restrictions . . . and legalized cannabis. Yesterday, thousands of people joined hands around Lake Merritt in affirmation of our differences, and to declare our intent to protect those classes of people who are most threatened by racism and harmful economic and judicial policies.

I am grateful to my coach and design editor Angela Lauria, who lovingly kicked my ass unlike I've experienced since Stanford's Associate Dean, Linda Paulson, bled all over my assignments in red ink. And to my line editor, Julia Kellaway, who upgraded this book brilliantly.

Thanks to Susan Scott, whose book *Fierce Conversations* inspired me deeply. I always remember her advice to me during one lunch years ago: Just write. Don't worry about grammar. Write incomplete sentences. Write to the soul, not just the mind. And read everything—not just nonfiction—but poetry, literature, and more.

And to my first coaches who put me on this path: Peter Vultaggio, my sage friend and guide during a difficult time; Judith Duhl, master coach who taught me (among many things) that you can have deep, moving, connections via telephone; and James Flaherty, who modeled how to live a brilliantly integrated life, and whose vocation has created thousands of integral coaches worldwide. James modeled meeting people where they are, and inspired me in his ability to adapt his style and methods to individuals. Heartfelt thanks to my current coach, HiC Lutmers, who helps me cut through chaos and stress to stay mindful and grounded, knowing what's called for in this period of my life.

To Jay and Jeanne, who came to my rescue, helping my daughter and I escape a lovely but toxic home that was poisoning me with mold. I could not have written this book with my mold-riddled brain. They prove that family comes in many forms.

To my parents and step-parents, who somehow managed to create a doctrine-free environment in the midst of a doctrine-heavy small town in Kansas. It was hard being different, but I'm grateful that I got to choose my delusions, instead of having them pre-programmed. I believe that I am more self-aware, less biased, and more open to influence and learning, thanks to your modeling of hard work, open-mindedness, and kindness to others.

And to my witty, silly, intelligent, warm friends who accept me as I am, and help me be my full, real self.

About the Author

Denise R. Green is a certified executive coach, speaker, and author who is passionate about helping her clients lower stress and improve their health, relationships, and effectiveness. With more than fourteen years' industry experience as a leader at Oracle Corporation and Charles Schwab, Denise understands the stressful corporate environment. Since founding Brilliance Inc. in 2008, Denise has coached and trained thousands of people in high-tech, financial services, healthcare, and consumer products industries.

Denise knows from personal experience what it feels like to go from burned-out to brilliant. In 1992 she was in a major car accident that changed her life forever. And, in case she didn't learn the lesson well enough, the universe sent her conditions including rheumatoid arthritis and Lyme disease. She knows how to achieve great things in spite of real physical limitations, and has devoted her life to helping others overcome anything.

Denise satisfies her inner geek through her study of applied neuroscience. Her knowledge of the brain and behavioral change allows her to help people quickly develop effective, lasting habits. She holds a bachelor's degree in French from Arizona State University (summa cum laude), a certificate from the Paris-Sorbonne University, and a master of Liberal Arts from Stanford University. A native of Kansas, Denise thrives in Oakland, California, with her brilliant daughter Katarina Renée and her wonder-mutt Andy. (Growing up, Denise once dreamed of becoming a stand-up comedian. To this day, her dream is to collaborate on a project with modern-day Renaissance man Steve Martin.)

You can find her hiking in the Redwood Regional Park with Andy, or at:

www.BrillianceInc.com

Denise@BrillianceInc.com

www.facebook.com/EvokeBrilliance/

www.linkedin.com/in/denisergreen

Thank You

Thank you for coming on this journey with me.

Throughout these pages, I've offered many tips,
ideas, and tools to make it easier for you
to become the person you want to be.

If you don't like pulling pages out of the book
(or squinting at an e-reader)
visit my website to grab free downloadable
copies of all the assessments and templates
in this book.

You'll find them at:
www.BrillianceInc.com/Resources.

Let me know how it goes!

Made in the USA
Middletown, DE
12 April 2018